UNDP

LESSONS LEARNED IN CRISES AND POST-CONFLICT SITUATIONS

THE ROLE OF UNDP IN REINTEGRATION AND RECONSTRUCTION PROGRAMMES

Edited by Rafeeuddin Ahmed, Manfred Kulessa and Khalid Malik

UNITED NATIONS DEVELOPMENT PROGRAMME

The views expressed in this report are those of the authors
and do not necessarily represent those of the United Nations
or the United Nations Developement Programme.

© Evaluation Office 2002

Sale No. E.02.III.B.12
ISBN 92-1-126150-3

Evaluation Office
United Nations Developement Programme
One United Nations Plaza
New York, NY 10017, USA

Design: Colonial Communications Corp., New York, NY, USA
Cover photo: Anish Pradhan/UNDP

CONTENTS

[1] The Development Programme for Displaced Persons, Refugees and Returnees in Central America
(PRODERE) was a cross-country, regional effort implemented in El Salvador, Guatemala and Nicaragua.

FOREWORD

In recent times, the developing world has experienced a large number of internal conflicts and crises resulting in widespread devastation, displacement of populations and tragic loss of life. Nearly all of the world's 20 poorest countries have experienced violent conflict over the past few decades.

UNDP and other development agencies have found themselves faced with the challenges posed in the rehabilitation and reconstruction of these countries in the post-conflict periods. They have also had to come to grips with the demands placed upon them in the aftermath of these conflicts on their traditional roles. Rebuilding of war-torn societies, reintegration of refugees, displaced persons and former combatants, maintenance of peace once fighting has ceased and prevention of the eruption of violence in areas of unrest are all taking a place on the development agenda.

Deeply involved in these issues by virtue of its universal presence and position as a trusted, neutral development partner in programme countries, UNDP has gained considerable experience in the post-conflict reintegration, rehabilitation and reconstruction arena. Building upon this foundation, it continues to examine how it might most effectively bring its comparative strengths to bear in such situations, in line with its mandate for sustainable human development.

In 1999 the Evaluation Office initiated a review of the work of UNDP in complex emergencies, with a focus on reintegration programmes. A team of consultants visited a number of countries, including Bosnia & Herzegovina, Burundi, Cambodia, Croatia, El Salvador, Eritrea, Ethiopia, Guatemala, Liberia, Mozambique, Philippines, Rwanda, Somalia and Tajikistan. Based on the team's findings, a publication, "Sharing New Ground in Post-Conflict Situations – The Role of UNDP in Reintegration Programmes," was issued by the Evaluation Office in January 2000. While reviewing the quality and impact of the reintegration programmes in which UNDP had been involved, it also looked at the larger issue of the role of development agencies in post-conflict situations. It recognized that complex crises and post-conflict situations, regrettably, are a significant and growing part of the developing world's current landscape, and that there are development dimensions at every stage of such situations. In particular, it focused on how UNDP's ability to make a meaningful and sustainable contribution through rapid action in such circumstances might be enhanced.

In 2001, a second evaluative study of Japanese-funded reconstruction activities in East Timor and Kosovo was undertaken. Both the 1999 and 2001 studies produced a wealth of country specific information and important observations of potential interest to the development community at large. This publication, based on the two studies and other related works, synthesizes and presents key observations and lessons learned from UNDP's involvement and experiences in post-conflict reintegration and reconstruction activities in different countries. While the situation in many of the countries visited may have changed since the missions were carried out, nevertheless, the present publication serves to contribute to the intended learning process in better managing the complex post-conflict environment for peace and development.

Several features appear common to most of the studies. The involvement of the UN system is generally welcomed in post-conflict situations given its impartial stance and even-handed interventions in peace building and reintegration. The UN agencies undertake a broad range of activities, extending from food distribution, demobilization of soldiers and rehabilitation of houses and infrastructure to de-mining, job training, organizing national elections and strengthening police capabilities.

Effective inter-agency cooperation remains a challenge. Strong commitment, well-formulated strategies coupled with clearly defined roles and responsibilities for each agency and reduction of bureaucratic impediments can substantially improve effectiveness. Overwhelmingly, there is a need to recognize that emergency relief, rehabilitation and development are not sequential, but that they must often be undertaken simultaneously.

Among UNDP's strengths, its ability to build capacities for improving governance, which greatly facilitates the reintegration processes, emerges clearly. UNDP, besides effectively implementing its own programmes and projects, has often been very successful in mobilizing donor resources for development programmes that fall within its substantive mandate of achieving sustainable human development. The need for flexible funding and robust administrative systems in UNDP country offices to address emergency needs rapidly is highlighted, as is the need to staff offices in the concerned countries with personnel who have had training and experience in operating in a post-conflict environment.

It is hoped that this publication will help to further the debate and lead to positive change as UNDP continues the process of re-examining its role in crises and post-conflict situations. The publication is the outcome of a collaborative effort by the editors – Rafeeuddin Ahmed, Manfred Kulessa and myself. I am grateful to Nuru Lama and Sharouh Sharif for their editorial and managerial assistance in making this volume possible. The contributions of staff of the Evaluation Office and other concerned units at UNDP headquarters who assisted in its preparation are gratefully acknowledged, especially Bibi Amina Khan, Anish Pradhan and Cecilia Reyes. Thanks are due as well to the editor, Mary Lynn Hanley, and to the designer, Julia Ptasznik. We would also like to express our appreciation for the factual validation and valuable comments we received from various members of the UNDP regional bureaux and country offices, including Babacar Cisse, Flavia Pansieri, Gany Diaroumeye-Sabatier, Hiroko Takagi, Janne Heiskanen, Kari Bleindheim, Ladislaus Byenka-Abwooli, Lamin Manneh, Larry Maramis, Luca Renda, Mary Symmonds and Sarah Poole.

Khalid Malik
Director, Evaluation Office
United Nations Development Programme

I. TOWARDS A FULLER UNDERSTANDING OF COUNTRIES IN CRISES AND POST-CONFLICT SITUATIONS: AN ANALYTICAL FRAMEWORK

INTRODUCING THE SUBJECT AND CONTEXT

Countries in crises and post-conflict situations (CPCs) can appropriately be defined as those experiencing or having suffered the consequences of physical confrontation between opposing forces. Going a step further, it is important to be aware of the shared characteristics of conflict situations, not only for the purpose of advancing preventive measures, but also to design ways and means of mitigating their effects.

The worst deprived societies, whether measured by human development indicators or GDP per capita, tend to have had major civil conflicts or wars. A staggering half of all low-income countries have experienced major political violence. Frances Stewart states that "crisis prevention is essential for poverty reduction, and policies aimed at reducing political violence are needed for all low-income countries, given their propensity for violence.[2]" Preventing conflict requires an understanding of its economic and social causes and the design of policies that strengthen social capital. In looking at conflict among organized groups, factors such as the economic and social differentiation (group identity etc.) and the political ambition of opportunistic leaders stand out. A basic reason for group conflict however is relative inequity and perceived denial of "rights." Prevention of conflicts requires countervailing pressures such as a strong state and/or communities. Dysfunctional social capital can easily overwhelm institutions created when society was more stable with less open conflict. Repairing institutions alone without a concomitant rebuilding of social capabilities is unlikely to be lasting. "Good" policies become insufficient if the government is not broadly based and groups do not feel appropriately represented.

---

[2] Stewart, Frances, *Tackling Horizontal Inequalities,* Proceedings from a World Bank Conference, World Bank, Washington, D.C. 2000

WHY CONFLICTS OCCUR?

Current literature on CPCs lists a variety of reasons why conflicts occur. The notable causes of conflict specified by Frances Stewart[3] comprise: poverty and unequal access to resources; a history of inter-group tensions based on religious/ethnic/cultural/ linguistic differences; denial of rights of self-determination; territorial claims, arising in many instances from perceived inequity of borders imposed by colonial powers; and the absence of credible national institutions to resolve differences. The various causes often overlap.

The four most common types of inequalities relate to political power sharing, glaring income disparities, unequal employment opportunities and social segregation. For violence to occur, the motivated groups must generally: share perceptions of inequalities at family and community levels; believe that conflict would result in increased benefits to them; be convinced that they could prevail militarily over their opponents; and possess the material and financial resources to engage in armed conflict. When these conditions are present, specific events or actions cause a simmering dispute to boil over into violent conflict.

WHAT ARE THE CONSEQUENCES OF CPCs?

It is estimated that, on average, over 300,000 deaths occur each year as a result of conflicts, and that an even larger number of injuries are sustained. Women and children (civilians as well as combatants) account for a significant number of the casualties. As small arms such as AK-47s, G-3s and AR-155s are the principal weapons used, along with landmines, participation in conflicts is easily broadened. Most of the casualties occur in developing countries. It has been estimated that "of more than 150 major conflicts since World War II, 130 have been fought in the developing world[4]."

Conflicts result in the related human tragedy of the displacement of large numbers of persons as war damages infrastructure, including roads, dams, bridges, dwellings, schools, health centres and agricultural land. Physical damage resulting from conflict costs billions of dollars a year. Beyond these grievous tolls, conflicts leave behind a legacy of deep and enduring social, political and psychological wounds. They can reverse decades of economic progress and impede future development. For these reasons, economic and social stability and human security become essential pre-conditions for sustainable development. As a World Bank report highlights, "Violent conflict, within or between countries, results in loss of life and destruction of assets, contributes to social and economic disintegration and reverses the gains of development, thereby adversely affecting the Bank's core mission of poverty reduction[5]." In the same vein, inasmuch as the core mandate of the United Nations Development Programme (UNDP) is also to combat poverty, Frances Stewart has recommended that the *Human Development Report* annually commissioned by UNDP incorporate CPCs as a key variable[6].

---

[3] Ibid
[4] Muggah, Robert and Berman, Eric, "Humanitarianism Under Threat: The Humanitarian Impacts of Small Arms and Light Weapons," A Study Commissioned by the Reference Group on Small Arms of the Inter-Agency Standing Committee, New York, NY, March 2001
[5] World Bank, *Operational Manual,* January 2001
[6] Stewart, Frances, Ibid

HOW TO PREVENT CPCs?

The critical importance of conflict prevention is enshrined in Article 1 of the United Nations Charter. In his report to the Security Council on the causes of conflict, Mr. Kofi Annan, Secretary-General of the United Nations, declared, "For the United Nations there is no higher goal, no deeper commitment and no greater ambition than to prevent armed conflict." Clearly the most important policy is one that seeks to reduce the motivational factors, notably group inequalities. For this reason, the *Report of the Panel on United Nations Peace Operations* (the Brahimi report) calls on UNDP to take a lead role in conflict prevention by addressing, through good governance, the structural causes of conflict:

(a) On the economic side, the policies should ensure moderate horizontal inequalities in respect to assets, employment and incomes;

(b) On the political, cultural and social side, governments, as ruling authorities, should share power with all the various factions in society and ensure their participation in the administration, the army and the police;

(c) With regard to justice, the rule of law should be promoted and the administration of justice should be effective and fair; and

(d) Human security should be ensured while strengthening accountable, transparent and participatory governance that promotes equitable economic growth, inclusive of social development and national ownership of development programmes[7].

The Brahimi report identifies UNDP as ideally suited to prevent conflicts because of its vast expertise and knowledge of local conditions in CPCs. In fact, UNDP is embarking on a global "Mainstreaming Governance and Conflict Prevention Programme." It will include support to governance institutions capable of resolving conflicts peacefully and upholding the rule of law through such means as the pursuit of justice following the cessation of hostilities, reform of the security sector and support to national human rights institutions.

As early as 1995, the UNDP/UNFPA Executive Board established a new funding mechanism comprising five per cent of its core resources (TRAC 1.1.3) enabling UNDP to address conflict prevention as well as the developmental and institutional aspects of rehabilitation and reconstruction. In the same spirit, the "Administrator's Business Plans 2000-2003" seek to strengthen UNDP capacities to lead efforts in assisting CPCs.

The 1997 *OECD DAC Guidelines on Conflict, Peace and Development Co-operation* include a comprehensive listing of preventive measures available under three scenarios:

In **situations of submerged tensions** activities should be aimed at:

■ improving the allocation and management of natural resources;

■ reducing poverty;

■ targeting socio-political activities in support of participatory development;

■ promoting good governance;

■ limiting the flow and diffusion of arms, especially light weapons;

---

[7] United Nations, "Report of the Panel on United Nations Peace Operations," August 2000

- civic education, ensuring respect for human rights;
- supporting self-help potential among crisis-threatened population groups; and
- creation of dialogue and mediation structures.

In **situations of rising tensions** it becomes particularly important to monitor and prevent the stockpiling of arms by the conflicting parties.

In **violent conflict situations,** preventive diplomacy and military measures, supported by humanitarian aid, are useful for moderating conflict, ending hostilities and starting peace negotiations.

HOW TO MITIGATE CPC CONSEQUENCES?

Professor Joseph Stiglitz, Nobel laureate and former Chief Economist of the World Bank, argues against "one size of clothing fits all" strategies in addressing development programmes. The OECD/DAC 1997 guidelines similarly state that "all complex emergencies are different and situation-specific strategies need to be developed for each crisis. A thorough understanding of local conditions is vital." These guidelines, *inter alia,* support the Brahimi report's preference for the involvement of UNDP, in view of its knowledge of country-specific circumstances.

There has been considerable thought given to how best to organize responses to mitigate the consequences of conflict. It is important that the main responsibility for planning and executing the recovery lie with the government, supported as required by the international community. Given its comprehensive and diversified nature (political, military/technical, security, humanitarian and socio-economic), the achievement of recovery requires the broad participation of many actors, working collectively. The UN agencies should make contributions on the basis of their mandates and expertise. However, they themselves do not possess sufficient capacities and resources to work without partners. Daniel Kaufman asserts that "for too long, economists have underestimated the importance of participation in development[8]." Other intergovernmental, regional, non-governmental and private sector actors also need to be involved. Coordination is an essential element of the work of the UN Country Team, preferably under the leadership of the resident coordinator, in line with the Brahimi report recommendations.

Formulating a programme for organizing technical assistance and financial support for recovery and rehabilitation is also thought to be important. Financial support could be mobilized from a wide range of sources: voluntary funding raised through consolidated appeals, special trust funds, parallel financing from bilateral programmes or regional organizations, and cash or in-kind contributions from national institutions.

Following conflict, the most pressing issue is to reintegrate former combatants, IDPs and refugees into society and enable them to engage in productive activities under area-based rehabilitation and reintegration schemes implemented at the community level. The purpose is to have disparate elements of the population work together, to cultivate trust, and to engage them in productive activities such

---

[8] Kaufman, Daniel, *Governance and Anti-Corruption: New Insights and Challenges,* Proceedings from a World Bank Conference, World Bank, Washington, D.C., 2000

as agriculture to improve food security, micro-credit schemes or infrastructure rehabilitation.

The USAID/UNDP Roundtable Report[9] underscores the need for flexibility within community-based programmes in order to allow for changes in the political and economic context, as well as for the different needs of each community. In order to be successful, the community should have complete ownership of the process in terms of deciding which projects to implement, based on its knowledge of local conditions. It should also determine timing and the funding requirements. A credible justice system should be built, as well as a security apparatus in which all sides can have confidence.

Other priority areas of support should include:

(a) development of new national human rights institutions to monitor violations, and of legal frameworks consistent with human rights standards;

(b) a focus on gender concerns, given the large numbers of women seriously affected by conflicts;

(c) creation of governance institutions capable of resolving conflicts peacefully;

(d) development of effective mechanisms for civilian oversight of the security sector, accountability and prevention of abuse and corruption;

(e) legitimization of state institutions through elections;

(f) fostering of communications among social groups in an effort to encourage the re-emergence of civil society; and

(g) building of administrative capacities through training programmes.

Additional important components could include environmental rehabilitation, to identify sustainable patterns of land use and establish local health systems with a view toward decentralized health and primary health care services; and the development of local education systems, designed, *inter alia,* to bridge differences within society.

EMPIRICAL ANALYSES BASED ON COUNTRY CASE STUDIES

Observations and recommendations in this publication are based on a study of 16 countries in crises or post-conflict situations. In the majority of cases, as in Bosnia and Herzegovina, Burundi, Croatia, East Timor, Eritrea, Ethiopia, Kosovo, the Philippines and Rwanda, fighting erupted as a result of perceived injustices and outbreaks of violence based on cultural and religious identities. In the absence of genuine power sharing, and given perceptions of intolerance and denied opportunities when one or the other group holds power, inequalities inevitably lead to conflict and violence can be triggered by unexpected events. Civil wars for independence were fought in Croatia, East Timor, Eritrea and Kosovo. In Somalia, rule by clans and the formation of regional-based enclaves has led to a failed state.

In most of the countries studied, ethnic difference was the key reason for conflict. Different political philosophies represent yet another cause, as seen in the case of El Salvador. In yet another case, in Liberia, fighting was initiated to

---

[9] UNDP Bureau for Crises Prevention and Recovery (formerly Emergency Response Division) & USAID Office of Transition Initiatives, "Community-Based Reintegration and Rehabilitation in Post-Conflict Settings," Washington, D.C., October 2000

counter income inequalities when some groups faced exploitation and hardship despite relatively abundant natural resources and an economically active population.

Characteristics of all of the conflicts studied include loss of life, human suffering and damage to the economy, property, infrastructure and social fabric. The case studies also refer to programmes required to rehabilitate infrastructure, notably in Bosnia and Herzegovina, East Timor, Ethiopia, Kosovo, Liberia, Somalia and Tajikistan. Such infrastructure includes property and housing, facilities for industry and agricultural land. There is also a need to replace livestock that was either destroyed or carried off. Facilities that often need to be provided, improved or repaired include water supply systems, electric systems, roads, health centres and services, and schools and educational programmes. Environmental rehabilitation such as reforestation and the cleansing of rivers is also necessary. Particular notice must be taken of the large tracts of productive agricultural land that have been strewn with landmines, notably in Bosnia and Herzegovina, Cambodia and Mozambique.

When there is ethnic disturbance, the social fabric of society is inevitably strained. In areas wreaked by devastation, the teams found increasing numbers of persons living below the poverty line, fully corroborating the close relationship between CPCs and poverty. In most cases the end of physical confrontation was marked by peace agreements that required monitoring by external parties. However in some instances, peace remained elusive.

Unless the underlying causes of conflict are adequately addressed, an agreement on peaceful co-existence and power sharing will not necessarily prevent conflicts from reoccurring. Conditions of security and essentials of revival cannot be easily established. Only through good governance and by providing equal opportunities to all segments of the society can the goal of long-term stability be achieved.

There is no set pattern with regard to governments shouldering responsibilities for mitigating crises. The situation in Bosnia and Herzegovina is unusual due to the existence of two government entities: the Federation of Bosnia and Herzegovina and the Republika Srpska. The international community has been obliged to take on additional responsibilities due to these special circumstances and the tensions prevailing among the two parties. In other cases, such as Burundi, Croatia, the Philippines, Liberia, Rwanda, Tajikistan and Somalia, the governments could not effectively mitigate the crises, either because they lacked the capacities or they were unable to ensure security to guide and implement relief, rehabilitation and reconstruction efforts. In such situations, programmes suffered from quality issues and implementation delays. In yet other cases, the governments themselves assumed lead roles in coordinating the mitigation of crises. Notable among them are El Salvador, Eritrea, Ethiopia, and Mozambique. The principal reasons why the governments of these countries assumed lead roles were that they wished to be self-reliant in the mitigation efforts, or that they possessed effective national institutions capable of responding both from a technical standpoint and from the perspective of interacting with the donor community on the responses to be provided.

The observation that the main responsibility for planning and execution lies with the government is fully appreciated and recommended. Initially, when new governments lack structures, UNDP and the UN system can shoulder increased responsibilities as in Cambodia, East Timor and Kosovo. In such instances, Joint Reintegration Programming Units could be established to implement new programmes. Such tasks should be slowly devolved onto government agencies as capacities come on stream. As required, UNDP can also assist governments in putting into place structures for coordinating and planning, such as Programme Management Units (PMUs), as well as Reintegration Programme Units (RPUs), Humanitarian Aid Commissions (HACs), and Relief and Rehabilitation Agencies (RRAs), as illustrated in some of the country studies.

The country studies also confirmed that partnership building is very important in CPCs in order to attain optimal impact. The essential conclusions are as follows:

(a) It is clear that UNDP should not engage in humanitarian relief operations that agencies such as WFP and UNHCR can handle more effectively;

(b) The respective roles of each agency should be clearly defined in Memoranda of Understanding;

(c) There should be a flexible and progressive shift from relief to rehabilitation to development without time linkages;

(d) UNDP's comparative strengths are in its country presence, acceptance as a UN agency with a generalist development mandate and related holistic view, and established relationships with governments and civil society;

(e) Collaboration by UNDP with other parts of the UN system is crucial for success during and beyond the early relief phase. In this context, the RC/RR is of fundamental importance. There is a need for him/her to ensure joint UN programming exercises for the preparation of balanced and comprehensive programmes, and in order to avoid duplication. The RC/RR also needs to establish a common trust fund with resources available to all major UN agencies. This can overcome their reluctance to enter into joint programming arrangements and thereby help to promote coordination strategies;

(f) At the headquarters level, there is a need for close coordination among agency headquarters, to simplify agency procedures and to delegate authorizations to in-country staff during post-conflict periods. In addition, the headquarters entities (e.g. UNDP regional bureaux and the Bureau for Crisis Prevention and Recovery {BCPR}) should effectively backstop country recovery efforts;

(g) International and national NGOs could be valuable partners to UNDP in many ways – in obtaining insight into and knowledge of local conditions and situations as well as practical problems of development management, in consolidating the relationship with bilateral donors, and in obtaining their support for UNDP activities; and

(h) It is important that donors ensure sufficient funding commensurate with the demands being faced by countries seeking post-conflict recovery.

Also, UN country offices properly staffed with professionals experienced in handling the special aid imperatives that arise in CPCs are required. Personnel involved in CPCs require different qualifications. Country and emergency experience becomes more important. Action, innovation and achievement need to be accorded priority over procedural considerations. Procedures regarding sub-contracts, hiring of staff, etc. need to be re-examined in the light of the specific requirements. The delegation of greater authority to the resident representative is required. A positive case in point is the signing of cost-sharing agreements, and the work of local contract committees. In this context, the loan to CPCs of staff from other duty-stations that have demonstrated the required competencies is of particular importance.

The country studies confirm the need to formulate a Recovery and Rehabilitation programme in order to mobilize resources. UNDP should develop a "special roundtable module" for use in government/UNDP resource mobilization exercises for CPCs. Here, the Rwanda exercise could be used as a model. Preparation (analyses, consultations, documentation, etc.) should be simplified. Emphasis during the roundtable presentations should be on explaining: (a) the need for and nature of short-term assistance requirements; and (b) how the proposed activities would serve as precursor components for development initiatives.

The country studies demonstrate that the essential purposes of programmes in CPCs are usually the same: to promote and strengthen the peace process; to reintegrate ex-combatants, internally displaced persons and refugees into society in a productive manner; to facilitate quick access by the target communities to basic services in such areas as health, education, water supply and sanitation; to initiate de-mining operations; to promote medium- and long-term processes of economic reactivation; and to enhance popular participation at the local level for Sustainable Human Development (SHD). The studies confirm the usefulness of the Community-Based Reintegration and Rehabilitation format, implemented by national structures for CPCs. This format has three advantages: it creates jobs for displaced persons and residents alike; it rehabilitates infrastructure; and it defuses social, economic and ethnic tensions. It is particularly important to note that successful programmes require a strong sense of ownership by the government due to sustainability considerations; the governments themselves should manage the relief/rehabilitation/development effort. Even temporary actions such as payments to demobilized soldiers or the creation of temporary employment opportunities through Quick Impact Projects (QIPs), such as those carried out by UNDP, contribute to the consolidation of political and civil society and, hence, to the sustainability of the system.

The following are the major substantive types of reintegration, rehabilitation and reconstruction projects undertaken in the countries studied:

(a) Economic recovery/development and technical/vocational training, both of which make it possible for displaced persons to work in the productive sectors of the economy, such as in agriculture or industry, plus provision of credit to enable thems to start their own businesses;

(b) Infrastructure rehabilitation and repair of transport, housing and other building infrastructure;

(c) Programming to address gender issues. A few of the studies demonstrate that CPCs necessitate and present special opportunities to introduce such programming;

(d) Provision of priority social services including health care, education, water supply and sanitation;

(e) De-mining. It has been demonstrated that UNDP has a comparative advantage in developing national de-mining capacities, and in managing trust funds for this purpose. This represents a new approach towards a decentralized model of international development cooperation. For instance, a Mine Clearance Training Unit (MCTU) has developed programmes in mine awareness, minefield demarcation, training of de-miners and implementation of mine clearance; and

(f) Projects that build capacities for improved governance. Such projects are needed to facilitate the reintegration process. This includes the introduction of human rights, including its economic, social and cultural dimensions, thus shifting the focus from displacement to one of general human development.

Certain "generic" lessons learned from experience in implementing projects call for particular comment. Flexibility is the single most important attribute for providing relevant, effective and sustainable rehabilitation assistance in post-conflict situations. This is true in all of the dimensions of planning, preparing and furnishing the assistance, including designing, budgeting, sequencing of events, scheduling, etc. Close behind in importance are well-structured frameworks for coordinating assistance, quick responses to critical needs, and the equitable allocation of benefits. Coordinated, quick and equitable actions sustain credibility and receptivity of the beneficiaries and reduce the risk of contention among them over the allocation of assistance.

The quality of post-conflict assistance greatly depends upon the quality of information available to planners. Comprehensive, accurate, specific and up-to-date information on economic, social, political and community conditions is needed for realistic, appropriate planning. Such information also helps to prevent unrealistic expectations among beneficiaries that can eventually lead to disappointment and resentment. As such information may not be readily available, measures needed to develop and disseminate it should be taken as early as possible.

Although post-conflict rehabilitation of infrastructure is not as urgent a matter as provision of emergency humanitarian assistance, it does need to be undertaken quickly. The wellbeing of affected populations, socio-economic recovery, and the credibility and possibly the viability of international assistance depend significantly on internationally recognized priority needs being met expeditiously. Institutionalized, fast-track processes that reflect the urgency of the needs should be applied to the formulation and approval of rehabilitation projects, and to the transfer of funds that will allow them to start. In the absence of such measures there is a risk that the process and time needed to implement the projects will result in delays. While such delays might be considered acceptable in cases of "normal" developmental assistance, in cases of post-conflict assistance they can greatly undermine the results sought by stakeholders.

Infrastructure projects are likely to face significant sustainability problems in places where ethnic or political groups have previously reserved management and technical positions for themselves, or where previous political/economic regimes have allowed less controlled societies and economies to acquire little experience with cost-recovery schemes. Thus, infrastructure projects are likely to require capacity-building and cost-recovery components to promote sustainability.

Post-conflict needs are likely to include the rehabilitation of various types of physical infrastructure. This can bring large-scale benefits. How effectively rehabilitation is carried out – and its positive results sustained – will affect the human security and development of the beneficiaries (typically numbering tens of thousands), the socio-economic health of many communities, and the speed and quality of overall recovery. Invariably this will require more than physical works programmes. In the post-conflict situation, the policies, institutions, governance and cost-recovery schemes related to the operation and maintenance of the infrastructure that existed prior to the conflict may be ineffective, ill adapted or non-existent. Thus, there is both an opportunity and a need for donors and international organizations to also address policy formulation, institution building, cost-recovery schemes and governance issues related to the operation and maintenance of infrastructure, and to capitalize on related "entry points" to address these broader developmental concerns.

Structured project management mechanisms, involving all stakeholders in a given project, can help offset complications surrounding project implementation in post-conflict situations. Project implementation in post-conflict situations is accompanied by uncertainty, the unexpected, weaknesses in coordination and information sharing, and relational difficulties among organizations operating in the same fields. This typically requires changes of plans and budgets. Structured, participative and substantive project management mechanisms, involving all stakeholders at working and senior management levels established and operating around a given project, can help minimize these detrimental aspects. In projects involving external funding and a need to obtain donor approval of changes, having a donor representative closely associated with the project and the other stake-holders is likely to facilitate and speed the donor review and approval processes.

The studies show that roles in project management should be clearly specified, commitment to carry them out obtained, and capacities to implement them fully assured. Typically, the formulation and provision of international assistance in post-conflict contexts places high demands in terms of time and performance on international organizations, many of which are likely to be under-staffed, under-resourced and over-extended, at least during the initial stages of their presence. National organizations are likely to be in a still more disadvantaged condition. In such contexts, it is all the more essential that all those involved in a given assistance project clearly understand and commit to their responsibilities, which should be detailed and accepted in a relevant project document or other agreement. If necessary, the ability of each party to play its role fully should be ensured by increasing its capacity.

Displacement and survival concerns linked to the past conflict can result in insufficient involvement of beneficiaries. Proactive efforts are thus needed for consultations through all phases of assistance. Typically, needs are assessed and assistance projects formulated shortly after the end of the conflict. At that time, many prospective beneficiaries of a given assistance programme may not have returned from conflict-induced displacement; or, for various practical reasons, they may not have known about, understood, or been associated with the international assessment or formulation processes. In "demand" type post-conflict assistance, consultation with beneficiaries should be a continuing process at all stages: selection, design and implementation.

Increases to project costs should always be anticipated. In post-conflict contexts, these costs are almost certain to rise for unpredictable reasons. There should be budgetary provisions to cover them quickly without affecting the quality of outputs or the initially envisaged benefits of projects. A contingency fund or budget line of a certain percentage over and above project budgets should be reserved for this purpose, and procedures set to enable expeditious review, and as decided, release of funds.

Even when international rehabilitation assistance is delivered expeditiously, from the viewpoint of the prospective beneficiaries there can be a long wait between the first contact with international staff, assessing requirements, and the actual delivery of assistance. Efforts are needed to maintain contact with and avoid the disillusionment of these beneficiaries in the interim. For this purpose, providing small amounts of aid early on is desirable, preferably aid related to the assistance planned.

The "visibility" of an assistance project, that is, recognition of it and appreciation for the quality of its assistance by those providing it, has little if any bearing on the project's success from the beneficiaries' viewpoint. For the donors and providers, however, visibility is a measure of success. But it should be understood as going well beyond the flags, stickers and signs publicizing the sources of aid. Visibility can be "positive" or "negative," or both, depending on a range of perceptions, including the usefulness, success, fairness and promptness of assistance. Maintaining positive visibility in post-conflict contexts requires attention to such matters as sustainability (vital to demonstrating the effectiveness of aid), regular consultation with beneficiaries, good information flow and adapting quickly to changed circumstances through flexibility in planning and funding.

Timely, accurate progress updates on assistance are needed to reduce misunderstandings among prospective beneficiaries. Uncertainty, confusion, a sense of insecurity and rivalries are inherent to post-conflict situations and can have negative effects on the prospective beneficiaries' perceptions of the assistance intended for them. This risk can be reduced through timely, accurate progress updates.

II. COUNTRY REPORTS

One of the early lessons learned was the insight that every stage of crisis and post-conflict offers its own challenges in terms of development cooperation. The idea was to find out what chances UNDP, with its mandate and instruments of development cooperation, would have to work towards peace and the reintegration of war-torn societies. As it turned out, the team could identify and recommend a number of concrete opportunities for UNDP involvement.

Among the key lessons learned is that humanitarian assistance and development cooperation are not to be seen as consecutive measures addressing needs in a process moving from immediate human catastrophe to reconstruction (as in the case of natural disasters). Rather, humanitarian, peace and development concerns have to be viewed in the totality of a specific situation and incorporated into a broader development framework[10]. While humanitarian assistance and development cooperation use different approaches, organizations and instruments, they also have much in common. Both have to orient their work to the overarching goal of establishing peace in war-torn societies[11]. Programmes to increase food security, rebuild infrastructure and generate income and employment opportunities provide immediate relief but they also form the basis for long-term development. It is thus imperative that organizations such as UNHCR and UNDP together be involved from the very early stage of planning programmes in crises and post-conflict countries.

Peace does not follow a given pattern in re-establishing itself. Everything depends on the historical, economic, social and political factors determining the specific conflict situation. In so-called "post-conflict" situations, peace may often turn out to be of a precarious and fragile nature. Of the countries visited, only about a third, now in 2002, can be considered as truly qualifying for the post-conflict classification, having overcome their involvement in war and violent conflict. Another third can at least be seen as less conflict-prone. The remaining third appears to remain in a similarly critical or even worse situation.

One cannot even assume that all war-torn societies are sure to move to a post-conflict stage, as much as we may wish this to happen. In reality, countries where conflict has reached proportions of endemic character come to our attention and the international community has to find ways to deal with such situations. The answer is not to be found, as some major donors seem to have decided, in a policy

---

[10] Stiefel, Matthias, *Rebuilding After War: Lessons from the War-torn Societies Project*, WSP 1999
[11] Anderson, Mary B., *Do No Harm. How Aid can Support Peace – or War*, London 1999

of limiting international involvement to humanitarian aid. This may turn out to be counter-productive in the long run. Solutions should be targeted to the removal of gross inequalities and inequities, which form the root of group conflicts. This requires a thorough understanding of the political, economic and socio-cultural conditions of the region or country, and proper assessment of the grievances and needs of the various groups, especially those not well represented in the mainstream political and economic structure. Ways must be found to give people a chance to stand on their own feet and to develop their own capabilities.

The country reports are grouped into two categories, countries in which UNDP activities were nationally focused and countries where they were mostly area-based. Programmes were nationally targeted in situations where the entire country was caught in the throes of a war, as in Rwanda, or when there was a strong government at the centre to allow for national execution (NEX) of programmes as in Ethiopia. UNDP was involved at the national level to manage elections, provide police training, strengthen judicial systems, improve governance and increase national capacities. Area-based approach programmes were targeted directly to communities or target groups most affected by war. The success of the area-based PRODERE programme in Latin America led to the implementation of similar programmes in other countries, including the initiation of CARERE in Cambodia. Many of the countries studied had both national and regional programmes with varying degrees of emphasis on the two.

CATEGORY ONE: COUNTRIES IN WHICH UNDP ACTIVITIES WERE NATIONALLY FOCUSED

REPORT ON BURUNDI

David Cough/UNDP

Rural communities rebuild while absorbing returning members.

Burundi exemplified the complexities of working in a situation where there was no simple linear progression from war to peace and from relief to development. In effect, conflict, insecurity, relief, rehabilitation, reconstruction and development were all occurring at the same time throughout different parts of the country.

In such circumstances, there should be no room for inter-agency competition regarding roles or mandates. Indeed, the cooperative spirit of the UN Country Team, planning, coordinating and implementing both humanitarian assistance and development support, under the leadership of the RR/RC/HR in Burundi, presented one of the most encouraging examples of synergistic action in a conflict-prone country.

I. CONTEXT AND BACKGROUND

In Burundi, politics and ethnicity have combined to produce a legacy of conflict and violence. In 1993, after years of authoritarian rule by a small Tutsi elite, the first democratically elected president, Melchior Ndadaye, was murdered, along with several high-ranking Hutu officials. The assassinations were followed by a wave of violence that led to the killing of tens of thousands of people from both ethnic groups. Subsequent insurgencies and counter insurgencies from 1994 up to early 1999 claimed over 60,000 lives.

As can be expected, the effects on the country's economy, infrastructure and social fabric were severe. External aid to Burundi dropped from $288 million in 1990-92 to less than $100 million (mostly humanitarian assistance). By early 1999, 550,000 Burundese were IDPs, while 300,000 were refugees, mainly in Tanzania. The IDP/refugee figures for Burundi fluctuated widely as many people left their homes at the outbreak of localized violence and came back as soon as the fighting subsided, in some cases returning only during daylight hours to tend crops and livestock.

Nevertheless, there was room for hope in Burundi. There were large zones within the country that were relatively unaffected by the fighting and were in the post-conflict phase. The Arusha all-party peace talks, which began in 1997, were given a fresh boost by the designation of Nelson Mandela as mediator.

II. RESPONSES

UN Collaboration

A single UN Country Team (UNCT) planning and coordinating group in Bujumbura oversaw both humanitarian and development activities in Burundi. The roles of lead agencies were clearly defined in key areas, especially those that bridged and linked the humanitarian and development sectors. Monitoring, evaluations, and field visits were undertaken by inter-agency teams. Under the leadership of the resident coordinator/humanitarian coordinator, the agencies approached and involved the government in their tasks.

The success of UN collaboration in Burundi stemmed from a combination of factors. There was the closeness of the UN community. Living in a small country and a delimited capital city, the agency representatives saw a lot of each other, understood where each "was coming from" and related well both on official and personal levels. Having travelled much of the country together, they appreciated the complex nature of a post-conflict situation and the folly of "going it alone." Because the amount of aid money all around was comparatively small, the agencies recognized the need to play to the strength of each other, to reinforce and maximize impact. As the then WFP Representative pointed out, "food aid is our resource, but we need money from others in order to move the food into position."

In Burundi, conflict, relief, rehabilitation and development were all occurring at the same time throughout parts of the country. The UNDP RR/UN RC, who was also the humanitarian coordinator (HC), had strong UNCT support in coordinating the peace and development process in Burundi. This was possible due in part to the team members being experienced professionals who had elsewhere observed the stalemate created within the UN community by outsized agency egos and empire building ambitions.

This is not to suggest that all had gone smoothly with collaboration mechanisms. The country team admitted that it had been a mistake to bring in an outside consultant to prepare the Common Country Assessment (CCA) report, which should have been an in-house exercise. Similarly, UNCT had opted for a "single fund" for UN programme activities in Burundi to promote cooperation and ensure transparency. However, it was later realized that such an arrangement was not possible given the legal restrictions. Not only was there no precedent for a UN mechanism to receive such funds, but accounting requirements of each agency headquarters worked against such a fund being set up. It was then decided to deposit the funds in an UNDP-managed Trust Fund.

UNDP Assistance

UNDP's portfolio in Burundi consisted of three programmes:

A. The Programme for Rehabilitation, Reconstruction and Support to Humanitarian Action (known as Continuum 1 and 2) and the follow-on programme, "Community Development Project Against Poverty." Implemented by UNOPS, the overall objective of the programme was "to help the country to coordinate humanitarian assistance and to support rehabilitation, reconstruction and re-launching of the economy." The target groups were, among others, the "affected populations in war torn areas" and the programme was focused on community-based activities including income-generating activities, with funding levels ranging between $5,000 and $10,000. The programme aimed at:

- supporting grassroots/community-initiated efforts for reconstruction;
- strengthening institutional and management capacities (of government);
- promoting agricultural production;
- promoting health; and
- promoting education for peace and national reconciliation.

In order to avoid the shortcomings of traditional sector-oriented programmes, which tended to be restrictive during crisis situations, it was decided to use a "continuum approach" which consisted of bridging the gap between relief and the rehabilitation/reconstruction programme. A progressive and flexible approach was adopted to regroup into one package different support programmes, which were complementary, thereby creating a synergistic effect. After 14 months of implementation, however, it was decided that this approach was too ambitious and uncoordinated. The Continuum 2 programme was then quickly set up with a simplified approach.

Continuum 1 was not evaluated before Continuum 2 started and as a result, lessons learned from the first activity were not sufficiently taken into account in planning operations for the second effort. A later report evaluating Continuum 2 activity underscored its drawbacks as:

- lack of precise implementation modalities;
- lack of precise definition of roles and responsibilities of intervening actors; and

■ problems in staffing and non-respect of staff management procedures and salary scales.

"Indicators of progress" had not been included in the original design, making it very difficult to assess the rate of progress and outcomes-on-track. Training accomplishments were meager, particularly for group management and programme management; for extension workers in technical skills; and for local management structures in programme design.

The "Community Development Project Against Poverty" (04/1998-12/1999) followed Continuum 2 and was also implemented by UNOPS. As was the case with the Continuum programmes, the Ministry for Planning, Development and Reconstruction was the governmental partner, with the technical ministries involved in their sectors of responsibility (Public Health, Communal Development, Interior and Public Security, etc.). UNDP contributed $6.4 million, and the Government of Burundi provided FBU 300 million (approximately $0.5 million). Thirty-seven UNVs provided technical assistance at the local level.

This programme focused assistance on the vulnerable – mainly war victims, female headed households and youth, regardless of their status as IDPs or returnees. The principal objectives were to empower community organizations to ensure: the sustainability of the economic activities initiated under the Continuum programmes; capacity building for the technical structures for the development of local planning and participatory approaches; and improved healthcare. The promotion of women's issues and peace education were integrated as trans-sectoral themes.

B. The programme, "Supporting the Implementation of the National Action Plan in Favour of War Victims." Funds for this programme came mainly from UNDP core funds, which contributed $1.7 million. UNICEF also made a contribution, of $190,000. The programme was implemented by UNOPS in partnership with the Ministry for Resettlement and Reinstallation of IDP and Returnees. Programme tasks were divided as follows:

■ UNOPS: management of funds; implementation of programme.
■ UNDP: disbursement of funds; monitoring of implementation according to plan.
■ Ministry: choice of candidates for jobs; set-up of provincial programme selection committees.
■ Others: choice of staff to be trained; elaboration of agreements with NGOs and institutions; steering of activities.

UNDP's contribution was intended to be of a catalytic nature. Other UN agencies came in according to their specialty: WFP (Food for Work), UNICEF (schooling, sanitation), FAO, UNESCO, UNFPA and UNHCR. The programme had a twofold objective: (a) to improve the capacity of the Ministry in the field of coordination, formulation of programmes, monitoring and evaluation; and, (b) to support launching of local resettlement, reintegration and development initiatives, targeting mainly returnees. The approach was based on the following principles:

■ free choice of reinstallation sites;
■ complementing efforts of beneficiaries;
■ real will of reconciliation; and
■ special attention to the vulnerable.

An internal evaluation carried out in November 1998 presented a generally positive picture of the results achieved. There were 7,000 beneficiary households, which exceeded the anticipated minimum number by 4,000. However there were shortcomings in the setting-up of the internal management system, as well as in programme and staff management. The evaluation report emphasized the importance of working with other agencies (FAO, UNESCO, GTZ) and especially with NGOs (Action Aid, ADRA, Care International, Catholic Relief Services, Tear Fund, World Vision, etc.).

C. The Burundi Community Assistance Umbrella Programme (1999-2000). This programme, with a total funding requirement of $14 million, was designed to help rural communities (with a beneficiary population of about 1 million) regain their livelihoods while absorbing their returning members. The programme's approach was "based on the integrated, sustainable concept of reinstallation developed collectively by the UN system and its partners." UNDP, the manager of the trust funds, used the direct execution modality for this umbrella programme – signing contracts directly with implementers, mainly international NGOs, national civil society organizations and UN agencies. All activities under the umbrella programme used a participatory approach, enabling whole communities to identify their own needs collectively and then play a lead role in meeting them. Thus, strengthening of both community and selected national level organizations, badly needed for peace building and reconciliation, were the priorities in the programme.

III. LESSONS LEARNED

Based on UNDP's experiences in Burundi, it was determined that consideration of the following points can have a major impact on programme success:

- the key importance of competent UNDP in-country leadership;
- the importance of a jointly formulated strategy paper by the UN Country Team;
- the importance of a progressive and flexible shift of emphasis (instead of abrupt change) from relief to rehabilitation and to development;
- the importance of agreed mechanisms and procedures for cooperation with UN specialized agencies;
- the usefulness of cooperation with NGOs at the grassroots level;
- the need for UNOPS to develop appropriate mechanisms and procedures to handle emergency and post-conflict programmes;
- the need for competent management staff in integrated rehabilitation/reintegration programmes;
- the need for a well-designed concept of capacity building at all levels, based on assessment of existing skills and needs;
- the need to identify, from the outset, appropriate indicators for measuring the impact of reintegration efforts; and
- the need for fast and easily disbursable funds for QIPs and umbrella programmes.

REPORT ON ERITREA

Eritrea gained its independence in 1991 on the battlefield. The leaders of the young nation were determined to follow their own path of development without heavy dependence on the international community for its views and policy prescriptions. Reintegration programmes mostly focused on returning refugees and demobilized ex-fighters, and less on IDPs. Even in the face of insufficient donor support, the Eritrean government and people, through their own commitment to getting the country on the track to development, were laudably effective in planning and executing their demobilization and reintegration programmes.

Refugees return following the war for independence.

Jorgen Schytte/UNDP

I. CONTEXT AND BACKGROUND

Eritrea, a former Italian colony, became independent in 1991 after three decades of a war of liberation against Ethiopia. This was a war of independence, not a civil war. The conflict ended with the victory of the Eritrean Peoples Liberation Front (EPLF). Victory was achieved without noticeable support from outside or any intervention from UN or other bodies in order to establish and keep peace. Neither was there any "failed" or "weakened" state. The EPLF provisional government simply replaced the former Ethiopian administration. A new conflict with Ethiopia erupted in 1998 and escalated in 2000. In the aftermath, approximately 1.1 million people had been displaced, principally from the Zones of Gash Barka, Debub, and Southern Red Sea, which are located in the south of the country along the border with Ethiopia.

Due to Eritrea's isolation during the independence struggle, the national government had little experience of cooperation with international organizations and foreign governments. It took some time for it to learn the rules governing such cooperative relationships. Despite the general state of destruction, post-conflict relief and rehabilitation was, however, relatively manageable in this small country, which possessed experience in relief transport and delivery to people in liberated areas. The restraining factor was the lack of necessary funds.

II. GOVERNMENT RESPONSE

As in all other sectors, the Eritrean government's reintegration policy was, from the beginning, based on the principle of self-reliance. It made use of existing institutional bodies, mainly the Eritrean Relief Association (ERA) and the Commission for Eritrean Refugee Affairs (CERA), which were later merged with other organizations and finally had their work taken over by the respective government ministries.

In the 1990s, little effort was made to support the 100,000 IDPs, even though small numbers of them benefited from various support measures aimed at returnees from the Sudan. The outbreak of armed hostilities between Eritrea and Ethiopia in 1998 produced a new wave of IDPs, even while the former caseload of returnees and IDPs had hardly been integrated. The newly formed Eritrean Relief and Refugee Commission (ERREC) had organized the return of about 170,000 IDPs to their places of origin. However, about 50,000 IDPs were still not able to return home due to the presence of mines/UXOs in their home areas, and because of security concerns in areas close to the Ethiopian borders. At the time of the study, 41,044 IDPs were still hosted in camps in the Gash-Barka region (including over 9,000 deportees). In Debub, 28,913 IDPs were sheltered and assisted in Senafe and Tsorona sub-zones.

As early as 1992 it was decided to demobilize 60 per cent of the armed forces. To help the disabled ex-combatants, the government encouraged and sponsored the establishment of the Eritrean War Disabled Fighters Association (EWDFA). Unfortunately, with the resumption of armed conflict in 1998, most of the demobilized (and partly successfully reintegrated) fighters were remobilized. A significant number of the soldiers were skilled and educated people and many others made up the agricultural labour force. It was expected that speedy demobilization, supported by reintegration efforts, would facilitate a return to normalcy for families and bolster the economic situation in the country.

Reintegration Programmes

Reintegration of Returnees – the Programme of Reintegration and Rehabilitation of Resettlement Areas of Eritrea (PROFERI). Immediately after liberation, the government conceived a programme – and tried to secure funds – for the repatriation and reintegration of refugees, mainly from the Sudan. Foreign governments and international institutions showed willingness to support such a scheme. First discussions with UNHCR and UNDP about a large-scale repatriation and reintegration scheme for refugees in the Sudan took place in July 1992. The provisional government asked that planned repatriation be carried out according to progress made in rehabilitating the sites that were to receive the returnees. But because of differing views concerning the terms of reference, a joint UN agency mission to Eritrea mandated to formulate an integrated proposal was cancelled. A 1993 pledging conference yielded a disappointingly low level of support ($32.5 million.) The government then decided to spend its own funds to carry out a pilot programme covering the period from November 1995 - June 1996 and addressing 25,000 returnees. Its purpose was to gain experience and use the expected positive results to convince the donor agencies to pledge sufficient funds for the ensuing phases.

After the successful completion of the pilot programme, a donors' meeting was again organized in 1995, presenting the government's proposal for the following phase, for which UNDP was assigned the lead role in coordinating all partners involved. The aim of the combined 1st and 2nd phases was to repatriate and reintegrate another 100,000 returnees between July 1996 and December 1997, at a cost of $83 million, which again could not be met by donors' pledges. UNDP contributed $9.3 million from its core funds and managed to solicit a Swedish trust fund for $2.05 million to purchase agricultural inputs.

The programme was concluded in 1997 with the return of between 135,000 and 150,000 refugees from the Sudan altogether, most of whom arrived spontaneously due to increasing difficulties in organized repatriation caused by tensions between Eritrea and the Sudan.

Demobilization and reintegration of demobilized fighters. In 1993, the Office of the President published a "Brief Summary of Policy of Demobilization," mainly based on the conviction that Eritrea's war-torn economy would not be able to sustain an army of 95,000 soldiers; and that the country's resources should be channelled to reconstruction rather than defence and armaments. Demobilization, considered a comparatively easy procedure, was entrusted to the Ministry of Defence and took only a couple of weeks. It was done in two phases – for the more recent recruits and for the veteran fighters. The personal data of the ex-fighters were given to the Department for Reintegration of Ex-Combatants (MITIAS), which was in charge of reintegration.

Unlike PROFERI, the reintegration of approximately 54,000 ex-fighters was not done as a comprehensive programme, but as an open-ended endeavour aimed at addressing the various needs of the individual combatants – training, job placement, psycho-social counselling, credit – without restricting assistance to a particular type of activity or locality.

The bulk of the funds came from the government and was spent mainly on severance grants, on a loan scheme and on various projects, like agricultural settlements and a mini-bus company. Foreign funding was exclusively given for reintegration projects, mainly from the EU, Germany, Italy and the U.S., in the amount of $8–10 million. European NGOs funded – mainly with money from the EU – skill-training programmes, a special loan fund for ex-fighters, agricultural settlements and various small projects, especially for women ex-combatants. Germany offered a two-year support programme of combined financial and technical assistance to MITIAS. As there were no special programmes for IDPs, some of those designed for ex-fighters and returnees tried to include IDPs, mostly women.

III. THE UN SYSTEM IN ERITREA AND THE ROLE OF UNDP

In the view of the Eritreans, the UN failed them during the post-colonial years, ignoring their plea for self-determination. In the beginning, this historic experience influenced the attitude of both the leadership and the people of Eritrea towards the UN system as a whole.

A first UNDP office was opened in 1992. A bridging programme, agreed with the government, was to cover the period from June 1994 to December 1996. It was followed by a Country Cooperation Framework (1997-1999), based on a government policy paper and aimed mainly at "supporting the government's key priority areas of human resources capacity development and institutional strengthening." Other members of the UN family present in Eritrea were FAO, UNFPA, UNHCR, UNICEF, WFP and WHO – considered as part of the "UN Development Team" – and the World Bank. As usual, the UNDP resident representative was also the resident coordinator. On several occasions, UNDP was asked by the government to take the lead in organizing donor meetings. In some instances, needs assessments were conducted by joint teams of the respective UN agencies involved. National execution (NEX) was the rule for programme execution with the Department for Macro Policy and International Economic Cooperation in the Office of the President acting as the coordinating authority.

Contribution of UNDP and UN Agencies to Development

The appreciation of the contribution of UN agencies, and especially of UNDP, has to be seen in the context of the attitude of the Government of Eritrea towards foreign assistance. Considering from 1996 onwards that it was time to shift from relief and rehabilitation to development, and to do away with conditionalities linked to grants, the government invited all foreign NGOs to close or phase out their programmes. This was concluded by the end of 1998. Simultaneously, most of the projects funded and implemented by foreign donor agencies came to an end, unless it was agreed that their funds would be transferred to the responsible line ministry.

The role of technical assistance was one of the bones of contention, as it was considered inappropriate and too expensive. The tendency of NGOs and bilateral agencies to execute "their" programmes directly, instead of leaving implementation to the responsible Eritrean authority, was unacceptable. The Eritrean leadership was well aware of the need for capacity building but wanted it to be directed straight towards the development of Eritrean human resources, and never substitute for them, in order to achieve self-reliant sustainable development entirely controlled by national actors. As confirmed by Eritrean authorities, most UN agencies – and especially UNDP – not only respected but also shared their attitude and tried to act accordingly.

Likewise, UNDP and the RR/RC found cooperation with the government smooth and satisfying, as they were working with serious and determined government partners. Obviously, it was not always easy to deal with the fiercely independent attitude of the Eritrean government. It showed frustration with UNDP rules and regulations, which did not allow operations to be as expedient and flexible as they desired.

PROFERI

For the government and UNDP, the PROFERI programme was meant to be a development solution to a humanitarian problem. It was designed to have a sustainable impact, to address the needs of the community, not only those of a special target group, and to deal with all sectors, not only with food and shelter. Its concept fitted the vision of an integrated approach to repatriation, rehabilitation and reintegration.

Regrettably, the size and success of the programme remained limited. Many reasons can be cited for this, the most decisive ones being the small level of donor support, the lack of experience of the Eritrean leadership and other institutional limitations. There was also a certain top-to-bottom approach, which could be explained by lack of time but did stand in the way of proper community participation, particularly that of women. Also, income-generating activities were usually not based on proper feasibility studies. Finally, the deterioration of relations with the Sudan contributed to the difficulties in organizing repatriation and preparing for rehabilitation of the returnees. Another more general weakness was the absence of practical and appropriate indicators to measure reintegration impact.

UNHCR and UNDP Performance

Eritrean government representatives had on various occasions expressed their dissatisfaction with the institution or mandate oriented approach of the UN agencies. In particular, they had been unhappy with the restrictive role of UNHCR in taking care of refugees only until they had arrived at the reception centres in their home country, with reintegration and even rehabilitation and the preparation of resettlement sites and support left mainly to the returnees themselves and to other agencies. The government had a more issue oriented and holistic approach than the agencies and became irritated when the UN system found it difficult to respond accordingly.

While UNDP's cooperative role in PROFERI was appreciated as respecting Eritrean ownership of the programme and trying its best to mobilize funds, there were still questions raised as to its role in leadership and coordination. Here as elsewhere, the concept of a "continuum" with a hand-over procedure did not suit the reality of the overlapping phases of repatriation, resettlement and reintegration. The general impression was that the UN system, for operational reasons and due to institutional constraints, favoured sectoral solutions where an holistic approach was needed.

IV. LESSONS LEARNED

UNDP's involvement in reintegration activities in Eritrea provide several lessons for improving its performance record:

■ There is a need for greater flexibility in UNDP procurement and disbursement procedures, rules and regulations.

■ In assisting countries in war-to-peace (post-conflict) transition it is critically important to provide early training and follow-up.

■ In multi-donor and multi-sectoral programmes, responsibilities for donor coordination and resource mobilization should be clearly defined and agreed upon at the outset.

■ Capacity building has to fit the absorption capacity of government and take place progressively.

■ Responses have to meet the government's expectations, and the government must aim at finding common ground with UNDP and other donors.

The PROFERI experience highlighted the inherent institutional problems of the UN family in handling repatriation and reintegration in an holistic and logical manner. Therefore, a few general lessons to be learned from this programme can be identified:

■ From the beginning, i.e. from the conceptual stage, reintegration must go along with repatriation, and it has to follow the preparedness of the resettlement sites.

■ The implementation of a repatriation, rehabilitation and reintegration (RRR) programme must be based primarily on the will to solve problems;

less on respect of the mandates of the intervening institutions (problem orientation versus mandate orientation).

■ RRR programmes must be designed with a long-term (10 to 15 years) perspective.

■ RRR programmes should not address special target groups (e.g. returnees, IDPs, ex-fighters) but communities.

■ Sectoral components (e.g. shelter, training, credit, etc.) cannot be seen as separate projects, but as integral parts of the whole programme.

■ All involved parties must participate in the planning process – the refugee communities as well as the local communities that are to receive the returnees.

■ Flexibility should be the rule: it must be possible to adapt and readapt planning and budgeting according to the flux of returnees, which rarely follows the figures of operational plans.

■ Demobilization and reintegration of ex-combatants has to be recognized as part of the general post-conflict reintegration task. UNDP should be available to assist the government in this field.

REPORT ON ETHIOPIA

David Beatty/UNDP

Demobilized soldiers march to the fields with farm implements.

Post-conflict governments are not necessarily weak. The case of Ethiopia shows that there can be a continuity of strong government control as a country moves from conflict to rehabilitation, and that this can be a welcome sign of self-reliance. However, aid agencies have to adjust and continually and persistently engage the government in constructive dialogue so as to encourage change in ways of looking at and responding to acute and chronic problems that require an effective and appropriate delivery of assistance.

Effective instruments of coordination had been developed and tried by UNDP and the UN Country Team in Ethiopia. The UN Disaster Management Team, under the chairmanship of the UN resident coordinator, provided the focal point for coordinated action and cooperation with government. The Emergencies Unit for Ethiopia became a major source of information and guidance in the field of disaster management and prevention and, increasingly, also in the areas of post-conflict relief, recovery and development.

I. CONTEXT AND BACKGROUND

In world public opinion, Ethiopia, one of the poorest countries, has been closely associated with disaster and emergency, particularly since the famine of 1984-85, which still stands out as one of the worst and most graphically depicted disasters of recent history. Although Ethiopia made a fairly successful transition from civil

Country Update

The signing of the Peace Agreement in Algiers in December 2000 halted the Ethiopian-Eritrean conflict, enabling the two countries to focus on reconstruction and development. In 2001 the ruling party, Ethiopian People's Revolutionary Democratic Front (EPRDF) went through a major renewal process with actions that included the reshuffling and displacement of some central policy members. Also, the Government of Ethiopia (GoE) went through a major reorganization of its structure, and rejuvenation of the conduct of its business. This included setting up of new ministries (for Rural Development, Capacity Building, Regional Affairs, etc.) with new ministerial appointees and reshuffling of previous Ministers, and appointment of a new President for the Federal Government. This rejuvenation and re-structuring was extended to the regional state level where presidents of most of the regions were newly appointed. Importantly, district level authorities were further empowered, bringing decision making closer to the ultimate target group, the rural poor. These actions of the government are expected to have positive impact on improved functioning of the government machinery and more effective delivery of services to the poor.

The World Bank developed a major post-conflict recovery and rehabilitation programme, which became active in 2001. The programme is comprised of soft loans amounting to $400 million and includes components for demobilization (up to 60,000 troops in the first of a two phase programme); reconstruction and rehabilitation in war affected areas (to support the safe return of IDPs and repair damaged infrastructure); a major de-mining programme; and a household recovery programme that would include recapitalizing small businesses or pastoralists, repair of housing and support for micro finance institutions.

In support of the government's development priorities, the UN system is involved in a variety of projects and programmes. These include: development projects and programmes in agriculture, industry, education, environment, health, food security, humanitarian and emergency relief activities, capacity building and governance-related activities (civil service reform and parliament). The UN system in Ethiopia is in the process of operationalizing its first UN Development Assistance Framework (UNDAF) as a means of encouraging greater coherence among UN agency programmes and expanding collaborative activities. The UN Country Team has adopted poverty reduction as an overarching goal of the UNDAF for Ethiopia, pulling together the concerns of all agencies to address the multiple dimensions of the problem and creating an opportunity to build close cooperation with Poverty Reduction Strategy Papers (PRSP).   Source: UNDP Ethiopia Country Office

war to peace in the early 1990s, drought, internal strife, food insecurity and the war with Eritrea have presented continuous and costly challenges on the country's road to development. The complexities of the situation require efforts to better understand and collaboratively identify local, viable lasting solutions.

The fall of Emperor Haile Selassie in the early 1970s and the ultimate defeat of the Mengistu regime in 1991 clearly established the link between political instability and the myriad other problems in the country and the region. The inability of both leaders to meet the needs of the people, especially with regard to alleviating poverty and food shortages, played a major role in their ultimate demise. This was compounded by the war with Somalia in the mid 1970s and the 30 years of war against the Eritrean liberation forces, fought first by the Imperial Government of Haile Selassie and, after his fall, by the military junta, the Derg. The war ended in 1991 with the overthrow of the Derg by the allied Tigray People's Liberation Front (TPLF) in Ethiopia.

At the end of the war, the Ethiopian People's Revolutionary Democratic Front (EPRDF), the civilian successor of the TPLF, formed the transitional Government of Ethiopia, which was in place from 1991-1995. The EPRDF dominated the transitional period through a combination of military power, effective organization and ineffective opposition. A Federal government was set up with nine regional states with decentralized governance. A series of elections at different levels organized in 1992, 1994 and 1995 laid the groundwork for the country's present decentralized system in which ethnically defined regions became partially autonomous. The May 1995 national elections ended the transitional period and consolidated the EPRDF's dominance. However, the various opposition movements, especially the Oromo political opposition, refused to participate in the political process.

As a result of the war and other disasters, the Ethiopian people have suffered numerous displacements, with over a million refugees and IDPs during the course of the last three decades. In the 1990s, Ethiopia simultaneously saw the return of many refugees and IDPs to their homes, continued displacements due to new disasters and the influx of yet more refugees from Eritrea, Djibouti and Somalia. In May 1998, hostilities erupted between Ethiopia and Eritrea. Thus Ethiopia's post-conflict reconstruction efforts became enmeshed with the effects of a new war. Before all the refugees and IDPs had been returned and reintegrated, hundreds of thousands of civilians were uprooted again and similar numbers of combatants were mobilized or remobilized. Thus, displacement continued to play a critical role in the country's development.

II. GOVERNMENT RESPONSE

As opposed to the situation in many other complex emergencies around the world, there was neither a failed state nor a weak state after the internal conflict ended in Ethiopia in 1991. The administrative structure at the central level had been left intact and, apart from replacing the political leadership and upper strata of civil servants, there were no drastic changes in personnel. Reintegration of returnees could therefore be addressed under the existing frameworks. Demobilization, however, was a new experience for the administration. At the end of the war, close to one million men had been enlisted in the various armed forces of the former regime, including the regular army, territorial reserve forces, regional special militias and police forces. Most of these former combatants needed to be demobilized and reintegrated into society, along with the returnees.

Reintegration Policy

The administration had a clear, though not formally articulated, policy concerning the reintegration of IDPs and refugees who fled due to war or famine. If the returnees were refugees, they benefited from relief measures implemented by UNHCR or by the Relief Society of Tigray (REST), which was supported by NGOs. Rather than targeting the returnees as a group, the new regime pursued a reintegration approach that addressed the needs of the general population, especially vulnerable people in the impacted areas. This was mainly done through area-specific, integrated rural development programmes and by combining the distribution of seeds, tools, livestock and food-for-work measures, which in drought prone Ethiopia, especially Tigray, have been common since the 1970s.

Disaster Prevention and Preparedness Commission (DPPC)

In 1997, the government initiated a National Programme for Disaster Prevention, Preparedness and Mitigation, financed with UNDP core funds. Up to that date, the

Relief and Rehabilitation Commission (RRC), inherited from the former regime, handled implementation of all kinds of emergency measures. The RRC was replaced at the national level with the Disaster Prevention and Preparedness Commission (DPPC), and at the regional level, with branch offices called Disaster Prevention and Preparedness Bureaux (DPPB). The original task of the Commission, as well as that of its predecessor, was to tackle the effects of natural disasters (not man-made ones) and to work on disaster prevention. The DPPC was charged with coordination work, including assessments, situation analysis and resource mobilization, as well as with direct project implementation where UN agencies and NGOs were not in a position to deliver assistance. The DPPC was also the focal point for Employment Generation Schemes, although the technical aspects of implementation were usually left to line ministries and their departments along with UN agencies and NGOs. At the regional level, the DPPBs were in charge of coordination, supervision of project funds and relationships with implementing and funding agencies.

REST

REST was founded by the TPLF during the conflict with the Derg regime in order to raise funds and coordinate and implement relief measures in Tigray at the time of the 1984-85 drought and famine. With the help of UNHCR, it played an important role in repatriating refugees returning after 10 to 12 years of exile in the Sudan and in resettling them, along with demobilized fighters, mainly around the fertile plains of Humera.

Though not a government entity, REST was a fundraising as well as an implementing agency. Its budget was around $50 million per year. With the overwhelming percentage of IDPs from the conflict with Eritrea assembling in Tigray, REST prepared its own worst-case scenario assessment, which was presented to the international donor community. REST's main partners were international NGOs, with WFP, USAID and EU providing mainly food aid.

Administration for Refugees' and Returnees' Affairs (ARRA)

Since 1989, ARRA had been implementing UNHCR funded and monitored support measures for refugees in Ethiopia (mainly from the Sudan and Somalia) as well as repatriation programmes. It was not dealing with reintegration of the returnees. Some of its major achievements were the repatriation of more than 130,000 Ethiopian refugees from the Sudan in 1991, a study for rehabilitation and reconstruction of refugee impacted areas in eastern Ethiopia, and the start of a programme of repatriation of Somali refugees to Somaliland. AARA had few contacts with DPPC and UNDP. Until recently, the field of refugees and returnees had been left entirely to UNHCR, which was funding ARRA.

Demobilization and Reintegration of Demobilized Soldiers and Combatants

In 1991, three months after the TPLF/EPRDF had seized power in Addis Ababa and the 500,000 soldiers in the army of the Derg had disbanded, the transitional government undertook the task of demobilizing the armed forces of the past regime, including the police, security forces and militias. The TPLF forces were established as the new regular defence force. Later, they were partly demobilized with a substantial group of them joining the new police and security forces and others included into various reintegration schemes. Armed forces of the opposition movements were also more or less peacefully dismantled and demobilized but did not benefit from reintegration support, apart from a group of former Oromo Liberation Front fighters.

The Demobilization and Reintegration Programme – the largest ever undertaken in Africa – was widely supported by the donor community, including UN agencies. UNDP, through the UN Emergencies Unit for Ethiopia (EUE), was involved in this exercise during early needs assessments and other preparatory measures, as well as in the delivery of agricultural inputs including tools and seeds for a significant number of the demobilized persons.

III. UNDP RESPONSE

The UN management counterpart of DPPC was the Disaster Management Team (DMT), comprising representatives of all UN agencies and chaired by the Resident Coordinator. In the conflict with Eritrea, DMT prepared a contingency plan that was submitted to the government as a basis for an interagency appeal for funds to assist the 350,000 refugees and up to 500,000 IDPs from the border areas. The DPPC also worked directly with the EUE through regular meetings, joint task forces, and studies and needs assessments.

In order to remedy the DPPC's weakness in financial accounting, management, monitoring and evaluation, and to prepare staff for their new role in disaster prevention and preparedness, a two-year capacity building programme was funded by UNDP. Apart from material input in the form of vehicles and computers, the programme provided for staff training in early warning methodologies and systems, establishment of food and non-food reserves, and management of a strategic transport fleet. Under overall guidance of the UNRC, EUE continued its support to DPPC by providing training opportunities and by initiating the joint development of information and data management software.

In leading up to the decision of the Boundary Commission and the eventual delimitation of the border with Eritrea, representatives of concerned agencies met with the UNCT and EUE to review scenarios and levels of preparedness for any eventuality, positive or otherwise. The secondment to UNDP by the Canadian International Development Agency of a Tolerance and Reconciliation Advisor who is based in the EUE has allowed for the elaboration of agency-specific interventions and plans for programming that will influence reconciliation at all levels but particularly at the grass roots of society.

In the conflict with Eritrea, DMT prepared a contingency plan that was submitted to the government as a basis for an interagency appeal for funds to assist the 350,000 refugees and up to 500,000 IDPs from the border areas.

Emergencies Unit for Ethiopia (EUE)

Though EUE always had a broader concept of its role, it did not function as a programming support unit for reintegration or post-conflict needs in relation to returnees, IDPs or demobilized soldiers in the transitional period after 1991.

In practice, more emphasis had been put on drought and emergencies rather than resettlement and reintegration issues. This concept of EUE's role was supported and encouraged by the government, which saw EUE's functions as information gathering, monitoring and dissemination for emergency situations, plus technical assistance to build government capacity in disaster prevention and preparedness. Ethiopia, with a cyclical experience of drought and famine, gave high priority to the prevention and mitigation of such disasters.

However, the EUE was also engaged in a number of exercises and studies that focused on elements outside the humanitarian sphere of its mandate. It was active in the identification of medium- and longer-term options (in conjunction with government and relevant UN donors, agencies and NGOs) that might offer a more sustainable and durable solution to the country's cyclical and endemic problems.

In the initial phase of the war with Eritrea there were reported to be 143,00 Ethiopians displaced by the fighting. EUE was instrumental in providing organization, support and follow-up to the UN assessment missions. It was also with the support of EUE that the UN Country Team (UNCT) pulled an Emergency Appeal together.

UNDP Country Programme Contribution

UNDP in Ethiopia had no separate reintegration strategy for war-affected populations, but rather responded to needs directly and indirectly through some of its other programming. Accordingly, UNDP programming was not developed to respond to the needs of such groups as IDPs, people involved in forced resettlement from Wolo to Tigray, Ethiopians expelled from Eritrea in 1991, demobilized soldiers and refugees from Somalia and Sudan. The area-based programmes were developed in response to food security and disaster prevention criteria, rather than post-conflict resettlement and reintegration needs.

As mentioned above, UNDP supported programmes that mainly focused on human and institutional capacity building benefited the community at large including in those regions affected with post conflict refugees and IDPs (e.g. Tigray, Somali and Afar Regions). In this regard, the First Country Cooperation Framework (CCF 1), covering 1997 –2002, between UNDP and the Government of Ethiopia (GOE) included a number of programmes dealing with Wereda (district) training for administrators on good governance and development management; food security and agricultural development; water resource development; the social sector; etc. The UNDP support for the social sector development programme (which is multi-donor funded) is focused on the emerging regions including Afar, Somali and Gambella.

Most UNDP projects and programmes in Ethiopia were under national execution (NEX). The NEX management structures had been integrated within the government structures and nationally tailored guidelines for NEX. The wide use of NEX can be attributed to the strong ownership and government control of policy direction and implementation of development assistance. However, to compliment the NEX modality, discussions with government resulted in use of direct execution (DEX) by UNDP for some projects including Mine Action and HIV/AIDS.

The UNDP Economic and Social Rehabilitation Development Fund (ESRDF) was a large programme ($120 million, World Bank; $36 million, government;

$38 million, bilateral donors; $7 million, UNDP/NORAD). The ESRDF was established in 1996 as one arm in the government's strategy to alleviate poverty. Its aim was to alleviate poverty through the provision of funding support to poor communities for the implementation of community based projects. The ESRDF focused on the rural poor and women as beneficiaries. Communities were given a greater chance to play an active role in participating in the design and implementation of projects and also in sharing part of the project costs.

The ESRDF's support focused on components like basic education, primary health care, water supply and sanitation, small-scale irrigation and capacity building. UNDP supported capacity building for effective use of the Fund as well as technical assistance to the management of ESRDF at both central and regional levels. The World Bank confirmed that this support was important to institution building. However, the Bank also stated that this demand-driven project received better response in the "better off" regions that had more capacity to develop and implement proposals. The World Bank was proposing a more equitable distribution of ESRDF resources through capacity building and technical assistance for the weaker regions and communities.

Support to Aid Coordination

UNDP co-chairs with the World Bank, the Development Assistance Group and chairs the DAG Core Group for PRSP (DAG-CG). UNDP convenes the Civil Service Reform Group, and in conjunction with the Speaker of the House, the Donor Group on Parliamentary Reform. UNDP participates in the Sector Development Groups and OECD Ambassadors Meeting. Support to the government's aid coordination mechanism and systematic collaboration with other development partners constitutes an important element of UNDP programme management. PRSP and UNDAF will provide the broad framework for a collaborative programming process during CCF 2.

Relations with Government

Government relationship with external donors and aid agencies showed improvement over time. The government supported and promoted the UN Country Team system. Particularly with the renewal process within the EPRDF (the ruling party), the government was much more open towards donor partners. Several key donors including UNDP were drawn to assist the government in developing the country's food security policy and strategy. The government also welcomed cooperation with donors on the Health Sector Development Programme (HSDP) and the Education Sector Development Programme (ESDP).

Response of the Country Team to the Ethiopia-Eritrea Border Conflict

It was difficult to know the precise number of IDPs from the Ethiopia-Eritrea border conflict. According to government figures, 500,000 people were affected and needed emergency assistance. In 1998, answering a government request to the UN Country Team, the RC and the UN Disaster Management Team went to work to ensure a rapid and coherent response. A "balanced programme of immediate intervention" for a total amount of $4.1 million was conceived and pledges for 77 per cent were received, in addition to bilateral and NGO commitments. DPPC and

REST were responsible for channelling the assistance to the needy populations.

In a war situation, the RC/UNDP RR was faced with new and unusual challenges. It was obvious that the regional peace and development initiatives in the Horn of Africa had become more difficult, including the plans for support for the reintegration of war-affected populations within the IGAD framework.

V. LESSONS LEARNED

Some of the key lessons learned from UNDP's experience in Ethiopia include:

- Strong government control can be maintained as a country moves from conflict to rehabilitation and this can be a welcome sign of self-reliance. Adjustments required by aid agencies in such cases may challenge the UN system's ability to react to emergencies in a coordinated, adequate, fast and flexible manner and can even threaten the agencies' principles of cooperation.
- Instruments of coordination developed and tried by UNDP and the UN Country Team proved very useful. The Disaster Management Team under the chairmanship of the UNRC served as the focal point for coordinated action and cooperation with government. In close cooperation with UNDP and the UNCT, the Emergency Unit for Ethiopia was a major source of information and guidance in the field of disaster management and prevention and, increasingly, also in the areas of post-conflict relief, recovery and development.
- The need to provide assistance to communities and through community structures was demonstrated. Rehabilitation and development programmes have had an area-based emphasis, focusing on affected communities and regions and not on specific target groups (with some exceptions for former soldiers and combatants).

REPORT ON LIBERIA

K. Diagne/UNDP

Women refugees on their way back from Guinea to Liberia.

The troubles that Liberia faced for a generation affected the whole population, two thirds of whom had to leave their homes as refugees or IDPs at one or another stage of the conflict. There had been alternating periods of relative peace and outright war. Like everyone else involved in assistance efforts, UNDP had to base its actions on the hopes of the Liberian people for peaceful rehabilitation and reconstruction.

UNDP was able to respond to crisis situations, offering coordination of emergency relief efforts and critical support for the resettlement of returnees.

I. CONTEXT AND BACKGROUND

Founded in 1847 by freed American slaves, Liberia was the first independent republic declared in Africa. From independence, a small elite of Americo-Liberians consti-

Country Update

The continuous fighting by dissident and government forces has eroded many of the gains that were made in the reintegration and resettlement of the population in northwestern Liberia. Recent IDP case load as a result of the fighting is estimated at 80,000. While most of the ex-combatants were rapidly demobilized without encampment, the hardened ex-fighters were absorbed in the rank and file of the security apparatus of the country. Many of these ex-combatants are being blamed for a good deal of the excesses and human rights breaches perpetrated by the security forces. The structure of the national security forces and the chain of command remain virtually the same as those of the defunct National Patriotic Front of Liberia (NPFL). The country is presently under a state of emergency with a discouraging security situation that precludes UNDP from being actively involved. The restructuring and training of the security forces along the lines of the Economic Community of West African States (ECOWAS) Peace Accords is crucial to lasting peace in Liberia and the sub-region.

The Liberia Five-year Medium Term Plan for Reconstruction and Development (MTP), which was prepared by the government with UNDP's assistance, succeeded the National Reconstruction Programme (NRP). The MTP contains several programme areas, including governance, gender, environment, and other Sustainable Human Development (SHD) concerns. It is the government strategy for reconstruction, development and poverty reduction. The resource outlay for the implementation of the MTP for the next five years is enormous and would require international support. Based on the overarching objectives of the MTP, the UNDP country office formulated a new Country Programme Outline (CPO) in 2002 containing two broad focus areas or "entry points": (a) reintegration and recovery at the community level and (b) capacity building for key government institutions and mechanism.

One of the success stories in Liberia has been the UNDP-UNIFEM led gender project, which has contributed immensely to raising the consciousness of the Liberian people on issues of gender equity. The project has supported the establishment of the Ministry of Gender and Development, and Gender Desk Offices in all Ministries of the Government. This has become the government's mechanism for mainstreaming gender in national plans and programme.　　　Source: UNDP Liberia Country Office

tuting only five per cent of the population dominated Liberian society and politics. Despite relatively abundant natural resources and an economically active population, indigenous groups were excluded from an equitable share in the country's wealth and disparities were widespread. Internal tensions grew with economic decline in the 1970s until a 1980 coup d'ætat ended the 130-year rule of the True Whig party. Although initially supported by the indigenous population, the military dictatorship that came to power was less concerned with addressing social inequalities than with reaping the benefits of power and favouring the promotion of the ethnic group of its leader, Samuel Doe.

In December 1989, a small, armed group, the National Patriotic Front of Liberia (NPFL), led by Charles Taylor, crossed the border from Côte d'Ivoire and launched an attack against Samuel Doe's forces. Within months, war engulfed the whole country. In the on-again-off-again fighting over the next seven years, no fewer than 10 factions emerged. While the ethnic affiliations of combatants during the war gave the appearance of an inter-ethnic conflict, the struggle had little to do with ethnic or liberation concerns. At its core, it was mostly about power and controlling the sources of wealth.

The human costs of the war were staggering: an estimated 150,000 war-related deaths; approximately 700,000 Liberian refugees in neighbouring countries; and from 600,000-700,000 internally displaced persons (IDPs). Altogether, internally and externally displaced persons amounted to more than 60 per cent of the total population. In 1996, only one of three Liberians was believed to be at his or her pre-conflict place of habitation. The use of adolescents as fighters during the conflict reached alarming proportions. All in all, the conflict devastated Liberia's civil, social and physical infrastructure.

Frameworks for Resolution of Conflict

The conflict was characterized by long periods of relative peace with each faction/party holding on to territorial gains. Early in 1990, the Economic Community of West African States (ECOWAS) and its military arm, the ECOWAS Monitoring Group (ECOMOG) attempted to mediate and finally intervened, alternating between peace monitoring and peace enforcement. ECOMOG's presence made humanitarian assistance possible, at least in the capital.

In 1993, the UN Military Observer Mission for Liberia (UNOMIL) was established and a Special Representative of the Secretary-General (SRSG) was appointed for Liberia. ECOWAS, however, remained the main actor in promoting peace negotiations. After many failed efforts, the August 1996 Abuja II Accords, endorsed by the UN Security Council, restored peace in the country. The Accords provided a timetable for cease-fire, the deployment of ECOMOG throughout the country, disarmament and demobilization of combatants, and ultimately, elections, which were finally held in July 1997.

II. RESPONSES

Demobilization

Some disarmament and demobilization programmes were conducted between November 1996 and February 1997. Of the approximately 60,000 combatants reported by the warring parties, only 21,315 were registered in the exercise, of whom 21 per cent were under 17 years of age. ECOMOG took charge of disarmament under UNOMIL supervision, while responsibility for demobilization was transferred to the UN-Humanitarian Affairs Coordination Office (UN-HACO). The UN-HACO decided on a rapid demobilization course without encampment and with limited reintegration support because a significant number of the fighters were part-time combatants, most of whom did not want to be identified as combatants after the war ended.

Government

As fighting neared the capital in June 1990, there was a complete collapse of national government. Over the next seven years, at least four Liberian National Transitional Governments (LNTGs) were established under different peace accords and with limited authority. In 1996, UNDP was able to work closely with LNTG-III in planning a Reintegration Programme. However, after the elections in 1997, slowness in government action at the local level delayed and hampered programme implementation and coordination.

The government at the time of this study was strongly promoting its National Reconstruction Programme. However, its actual capacity remained extremely limited. With the economy in severe disarray, internal capacity to provide adequate basic needs for the population and to absorb returnees, IDPs and demobilized ex-combatants remained weak. Internationally, there was much scepticism regarding Liberia's prospects for maintaining peace and achieving good governance; and donors were reluctant to get involved.

UN System Response

In the early years of the conflict, the RR/RC was appointed as the UN Special Coordinator (UNSCOL) to coordinate activities of the entire UN system, as well as humanitarian organizations in Liberia. During these years, UNSCOL had its strong and weak periods, mainly depending on changes in personalities involved, government relations and the security situation. This was true with regard to early planning for transition and reintegration. After the appointment of the SRSG and the establishment of UN-HACO, UNDP's role in coordination was reduced. Liberia's situation allowed for development activities to continue in many parts of the country despite the conflict. UNDP continued to carry its RC functions in respect of the support activities in the non-conflict regions of Liberia. The evacuation of all UN staff when the 1996 ("April 6th") war reached the capital led to a critical loss of property and records in UN offices, including UNDP's.

UNHCR and Refugees

UNHCR had been involved with Liberian refugees in Guinea and Côte d'Ivoire from a very early stage. Repatriation assistance began in late 1997 and continued through 1999. At the time of this study, over 80,000 refugees had been assisted in returning to Liberia and another 125,000 had been registered for voluntary repatriation. In addition, refugees were beginning to repatriate spontaneously in significant numbers. UNHCR was also engaged in providing reintegration support to returning refugees, principally through Quick Impact Projects (QIPs), mostly involving schools, clinics and water and sanitation.

Although there was continuous interaction and exchange of information between UNDP and UNHCR, coordination between the two agencies could have been much better. Moreover, the exit strategy for the UNHCR had not been well articulated and this was exacerbated by the lack of adequate funding to close the re-integration gap. An MoU was signed – mainly on joint project operational centres (POCs) – but not implemented.

III. UNDP RESPONSE

Emergency Response and Post-Conflict Planning and Coordination

In the early stages of the conflict, UNDP, under the auspices of UNSCOL, became heavily involved in emergency and relief coordination. In the absence of a normal country programme, UNDP operated on a project-by-project basis from 1990-1998, responding to needs as they arose. One of the earliest actions was a project intended to meet immediate field needs during the emergency phase. This project provided support to the UN system as a whole and assisted the RR in overall coordination of relief activities. It was followed by a project supporting humanitarian assistance coordination and serving the needs of IDPs, and later those of ex-combatants as well. It showed remarkable flexibility in responding to emerging challenges and attracting donor contributions.

Planning for transitional and reintegration activities began at an early stage, well before the actual end of hostilities. UNDP played a lead role with other UN agencies in supporting the process. In 1995-96, a new integration strategy was formulated with a strong contribution from UNDP. Looking back at this experience, the resulting Reintegration Programme was more donor driven than owned by the weak government authorities. After the 1997 elections, emphasis shifted to the National Reconstruction Programme, which was based on national initiative to a much greater extent, and again, received UNDP support from its early planning stage.

The Reintegration Programme (RP)

The RP, as envisaged in 1996, had four core components: resettlement assistance; restoration of basic infrastructure; counselling, training and employment creation; and support for elections. Instead of specific programmes for target groups, the focus of the RP was on rebuilding communities and promoting community initiatives and self-reliance.

The RP outlined a number of structures for coordination, including the National Steering Committee for Reintegration (REINCOM). At the local level, Local Area Task Forces (LATFs) were to be established as the local planning and coordinating bodies, to be served by Area Reintegration and Development Units (ARDUs).

The implementation of the RP was hindered by several factors: UNDP had less than expected success in resource mobilization due to lack of donor confidence in what was seen as a shaky peace agreement; county administrative staff were not deployed quickly enough to work with implementing agencies at the local level; the national coordinating structure faltered and was finally abandoned. The biggest problem was probably the lack of ownership on the part of the Liberian authorities.

UNDP's flagship programme in the RP was "Micro-project Support for Resettlement and Reintegration." Its focus was on entire communities in areas with the highest concentration of returnees. It was to be community based, participatory and demand driven, with initiatives coming from the people in the targeted areas. However, the programme could not achieve the desired impact because of its elaborate conceptual design, and in terms of the coordination structures on which implementation was to depend. Contradictions existed that pitted demands for rapid programme delivery against the need to pursue a participatory process. Resulting differences between UNDP and the executing agency, UNOPS, were not reconciled. It turned out to be difficult to keep the commitment to support only ideas coming forward from local initiatives when some of the communities of returnees were not yet assembled adequately enough to participate effectively. Thus, the implementation process stagnated. What was missing from the UNDP side was a comprehensive programme review, which was necessary to arrive at a consensus for an implementation plan that would take into consideration the still evolving conditions in the country.

Another example was the UNDP/ILO project of vocational training for employment and self-employment (1996-99). It provided short-term training in simple skills for 7,500 returnees, starter tool kits and support for cooperative business enterprises. While its success was limited because of the short duration of training and lack of employment opportunities, the experience gained was useful in designing a refined strategy for the following NRP period.

Despite the shortcomings, UN activities, including UNDP projects begun in the framework of the RP, contributed to the transition process through their engagement in the demobilization and reintegration of ex-combatants, stabilization of the pre-election environment, resettlement of IDPs, and revitalization of rural infrastructures and capacity building.

The National Reconstruction Programme (NRP)

After the elections, and with the government shifting focus from the RP to the NRP, UNDP was able to position itself to provide technical assistance while navigating through a difficult situation, acknowledging the problems with the RP and working closely with the government to develop a new alternative framework for the transitional period. The result was a reconstruction programme that had a great deal of government ownership and support. The NRP, instead of replacing the RP, subsumed most of its positive elements. UNDP played an important role in the negotiations concerning the contents of the NRP, assisted the government in its preparation and was instrumental in organizing the donors' conference in Paris in April 1998. This meeting succeeded in achieving pledges for the originally intended amount of $230 million. Much of this was not new money pledged but transfer of funds from RP to the NRP.

Governance

Under a number of projects, UNDP addressed issues of governance, mostly in the context of aiding the transition from war to peace. Though its support was minor in relation to the larger contributions of other donors, the UNDP funded a project of support for the elections and can claim some of the credit for their success. The Micro-project Support Programme also had governance components, which failed to materialize. Another project, "Strengthening Key Government Institutions in the Recovery Process," addressed the government's immediate technical needs with advisors and expert technical assistance, mainly supporting the Ministry of Planning and Economic Affairs.

Gender

None of the initial projects supported by UNDP during the emergency or transitional phase had a specific gender focus or component. In some cases, women and children were referred to or included in "vulnerable groups." Unfortunately, gender issues were ignored or not considered relevant. This was odd considering the primary target was IDPs, a group in which women and children were disproportionately represented. Indirectly, though not explicitly singled out in the project's objectives, women had become the major beneficiaries of several UNDP-supported activities in the reintegration context, specifically the micro-grant and micro-credit activities and some vocational training.

It was probably in response to this gap that the position of a gender focal point was established in the humanitarian assistance coordination project. More importantly, UNDP in conjunction with UNIFEM launched a gender-focused project in 1997 and further developed it in 1999 under the first Country Cooperation Framework (CCF). It was evident that many opportunities were lost with the failure to include a gender perspective earlier on in some of the transitional and reintegration activities. There was a growing recognition that civil conflicts presented a window of opportunity for addressing concerns of disadvantaged groups. It was known that in these situations, women and youth played important roles in community leadership and in the survival of the family unit. Roles that are normally resisted in tradition-bound societies, such as the involvement of women in decision-making on community priorities, are accepted in these cases. The later rollout of gender-specific projects made a significant contribution to promoting gender sensitization and to laying the foundations for gender mainstreaming.

IV. LESSONS LEARNED

- UNDP in Liberia demonstrated that it can effectively respond to crisis situations and be the focal point for the coordination of emergency relief and rehabilitation efforts, and in addressing the needs and resettlement of IDPs.
- Flexible project design and creative management will allow UNDP to respond to emerging needs by channelling or diverting funds through existing projects.
- Some of the plans and project designs prepared by UNDP had overly elaborate concepts and coordination structures, assuming too much about the Liberian environment, which was evolving and still very fluid.
- In the post-conflict context in particular, when a new project is started there should be close coordination between UNDP and the project implementer or CTA so as to arrive at a consensus on implementation appropriate for the changing reality in the country.
- Even in the case of failed or weak states, projects for which government authorities do not have a strong sense of ownership will be less likely to succeed.
- Expectations of "participation" in communities of newly returned re-settlers should be carefully examined as some communities may not yet be adequately assembled to participate effectively and reflect on community needs.
- Where possible, the identity of ex-combatants as a special group should be de-emphasized. In the demobilization process, ex-combatants should be encouraged to disperse rather than concentrate.
- In crisis situations, the RR/RC function is of key importance in taking the leadership in coordinating the humanitarian and development efforts.
- Regional bodies such as ECOWAS can make important contributions to peace making.
- Post conflict situations not only necessitate but even present special opportunities to introduce programming to address gender issues.

REPORT ON MOZAMBIQUE

David Gough/UNDP

Community members work together to rebuild.

Mozambique presents an outstanding example of post-conflict reintegration and reconstruction. Though UNDP's role and performance fluctuated during the periods of civil war and peace building, the organization was able to render a valuable contribution in resource mobilization and aid coordination, in projects of capacity building in the field of governance, and to some extent also in reintegration and area development schemes.

I. CONTEXT AND BACKGROUND

After independence from Portugal in 1975, the new Government of Mozambique (Frelimo – Frente de Libertacao de Mocambique) undertook a campaign to oppose minority rule in the region, providing assistance to liberation movements in the neighbouring countries of South Africa and what was then Rhodesia. In response, these countries engaged in direct military intervention and organized the formation of Renamo (Resistencia Nacional Mocambicana) with the objective of weakening and destabilizing Mozambique. An agreement in 1984, in which South Africa pledged to, but did not, end its assistance to Renamo, failed to end the war. Increased international pressure on South Africa in the late 1980s led to the cessation of all support to Renamo. The realization that Renamo could not prevail militarily, and reforms and political concessions on the part of the government, set the stage for a series of negotiations sponsored by Catholic organizations that eventually led to the General Peace Agreement (GPA) of October 1992. With drought affecting the entire southern African region at that time, there was also a mounting humanitarian crisis in Mozambique.

Three Key Features

Three aspects of the post-conflict situation in Mozambique need to be borne in mind when making an assessment of UNDP's role in the country. First, the General Peace Agreement (GPA) had been implemented relatively successfully. The success can be attributed to both Frelimo and Renamo's commitment to make the GPA work and to external factors such as the extensive support received from donors. Local communities in Mozambique appeared to be a primary force in further propelling the Mozambican peace process. The UN played a modest role in bringing about the GPA but the objectivity and neutrality of the UN enabled it to perform an important negotiating and arbitrating function, and to help build critical institutions essential to continuing peace and stability in Mozambique.

The second important feature is that Mozambique had attempted to manage the post-conflict reconciliation phase through community-based approaches. Four to five million people (nearly one-third of the total population) had either sought refuge abroad or were internally displaced. In the Mozambican situation there was no significant distinction between refugees and internally displaced persons

Country Update

Mozambique has made significant progress in recent years, notably the introduction of political pluralism and the adoption of market-based economic policies, including far-reaching structural reforms through liberalization and privatization. The net result has been rapid economic growth and macroeconomic stability over the last decade. The country's participation in the Enhanced Highly Indebted Poor Countries (E-HIPC) facility has also reduced its external debt from $2.7 billion to about $800 million in current net value terms.

The achievements on the macroeconomic front notwithstanding, the country continues to face several development challenges, including the need to maintain high growth, reduce widespread poverty, strengthen democracy and political stability, reduce unemployment levels, enhance gender equality in political as well as economic life, reduce the high incidence of HIV/AIDS and reduce vulnerability to natural calamities. The HIV epidemic in particular is emerging as a major development threat, affecting approximately 16 per cent of the adult population. The government's strategy to address the problem of widespread poverty is articulated in its Action Plan for the Reduction of Absolute Poverty (PARPA), whose medium-term goal is to reduce the incidence of absolute poverty by 30 per cent within the decade, and by a further 20 per cent by 2015, in order to meet the Millenium Summit targets.

The Second Country Cooperation Framework for Mozambique (2002-2006) was approved by the UNDP Executive Board in September 2001. UNDP's main areas of intervention will be poverty reduction, promotion of democratic governance and vulnerability reduction. To reduce poverty, UNDP support will include: strengthening the regulatory framework for enterprise promotion; and mitigating the socio-economic impact of HIV/AIDs. To promote democratic governance, UNDP will: support decentralization through capacity building for participatory planning and management at provincial and district levels and policy changes based on lessons learned; strengthen the Ministry of Planning and Finance in poverty policy formulation, monitoring and evaluation, budget review at central and decentralized levels and incorporation of poverty dimensions into macro economic policy and planning instruments; strengthen the parliament for legislative oversight; and strengthen the police and other relevant institutions, including the independent media. To reducevulnerability, continued assistance will be provided to improve coordination capacity for natural disaster preparedness and mitigation and mine clearance.   Source: UNDP Regional Bureau for Africa

(IDPs), as refugees only moved just across the border to other countries and most of them kept fairly close contact with their places of origin. Once the GPA was signed, both refugees and IDPs moved back to their homes or to other places in Mozambique, mostly on their own accord. To no significant degree did UN agencies, such as UNHCR, or other humanitarian bodies "manage" the process of return. It was largely an automatic and autonomous response, and it was estimated that 80 per cent of the refugees returned without any assistance from UNHCR. Reintegration and re-absorption activities were introduced later, targeting the general population without making distinctions among refugees, IDPs and demobilized soldiers. UNDP continually insisted on not labelling and targeting reintegration efforts to those in the three categories but also identified people who had remained in the villages as a fourth and significant category of people, and advocated for a category-blind, community-based approach to reintegration.

The third important feature of the post-conflict situation was that donors were highly supportive of the Mozambican peace effort and helped facilitate the task of the government in implementing the GPA. Significant donor resource contributions, both financial and human, facilitated the transition from conflict to peace, and consequently to development. Access to significant donor resources also enabled UNDP to play an important role in their management, at least in selected areas.

II. THE ROLE OF UNDP

UNDP activities in the 10-to-15 years prior to 1999 can be viewed as consisting of three distinctive phases. In the first phase, before 1992, UNDP was a key actor – along with the government – in managing emergency and relief operations. The UNDP RR was the UN's Special Coordinator for Emergency and Relief Operations (UNSCERO) in charge of the coordination of humanitarian assistance in the country. The government had expressly stated that there was a productive relationship with UNDP at the time. UNDP's involvement in humanitarian assistance enabled a link to be established between that aspect of UN operations and UNDP's development activities.

The second phase can be seen as starting in December 1992, with the establishment of the United Nations Operations in Mozambique (UNOMOZ) to oversee the implementation of the GPA. Alongside UNOMOZ, the UN Office for Humanitarian Assistance Coordination in Mozambique (UNOHAC) was established. UNOHAC had responsibility for refugee repatriation, resettlement of IDPs and reintegration of demobilized soldiers, apart from other relief and emergency operations. These two entities (UNOMOZ and UNOHAC) functioned until late 1994, when they were both phased out. The UN was seen as a political actor with peace keeping and humanitarian functions. During this period, UNDP was largely a marginal actor and the developmental role of the UN was also marginal. It should, however, be noted that during the two years when UNOMOZ and UNOHAC were functional, UNDP did play an important role in building up its capacity to deal with some urgent issues, notably the implementation of the electoral process and the reintegration of the demobilized soldiers. The RC, during the same time period, played a significant leadership role in coordinating the donor community in a situation where most operations depended heavily on donor funding (elections, reintegration, etc.).

The third phase started with the disbanding of UNOMOZ and UNOHAC, whose remaining responsibilities were taken over by UNDP. The UN resident coordinator function gained increased importance and UNDP itself emerged as a key actor in reintegration activities in Mozambique. There were several areas in which UNDP gradually established a comparative advantage under the unique circumstances of Mozambique, particularly in the area of governance, where UNDP had a built-in advantage in terms of its objectivity and neutrality. UNDP also played an important role in mobilizing resources and in managing donor inputs. Within the UN Development Assistance Framework (UNDAF), for which Mozambique was a pilot country, UNDP had an opportunity to work in close coordination with other development partners.

As was observed, there were many transitions from one phase to the other – from development and humanitarian concerns, to political negotiations and settlement and back again to a humanitarian and development focus. UNHCR, which had been active in the countries providing asylum to Mozambican refugees, had a brief period of active engagement within Mozambique with the return of refugees subsequent to 1992. During this period, UNHCR implemented numerous Quick Impact Projects (QIPs). Many development practitioners held the view that greater consultation by UNHCR on QIPs could have enabled the incorporation of elements essential to their long-term sustainability. However, there was also argument that the urgency to act did not leave much room for wider considerations. When refugees and IDPs returned, immediate action had to be taken to address their needs. Their centres of residence at such times were often of a temporary rather than a permanent nature, making long-term planning tricky.

The "hand-over" of UNHCR activities was another issue. It was not mandated that UNDP take over all QIP activities, although taking responsibility for projects that fit in with its long-term development programmes would be appropriate. The real role for UNDP, looking at experiences in Mozambique and elsewhere, should have been to liase with UNHCR so that there could be a coordinated follow-up to QIP types of activities when necessary. What was required was not a hand-over procedure, but a joint effort to facilitate a smooth transition from relief operations to development. This implies the need for UNHCR to involve development partners such as UNDP and donors from the early stages of the reintegration process.

Key Activities of UNDP

As noted above, in Mozambique, development and humanitarian assistance programmes, including those of UNDP, had not targeted refugees, IDPs and demobilized soldiers separately, with the exception of one project that required direct assistance to demobilized soldiers. However, many UNDP projects did have important implications for these three categories of people and their reintegration, as well as for generally managing the post-conflict transition to peace and development. Just as the breakdown of law and order leads to refugee situations and internal displacement, the re-establishment of law and order, on a sustainable basis, is a critical task for UNDP in post-conflict situations, necessary to bring peace and create a congenial framework for development. In Mozambique, UNDP's comparative advantage was in the area of governance; it was significantly less marked in fields such as area development.

The experience in Mozambique clearly points to the overarching significance of governance issues in post-conflict situations. Functioning legislative assemblies, the legitimacy of the electoral process, and the objectivity and efficiency of the judiciary, the judicial system and the police are key factors in consolidating peace and establishing the basic pre-conditions for development. These are also highly sensitive areas, where external interventions have to be mediated through bodies seen as objective and neutral, such as UNDP. In Mozambique, UNDP was building up an impressive track record in this area as both government and donors reached out to it to manage projects and programmes for building up governance capacities.

Reintegration Support Scheme. One of the earliest post-conflict tasks of UNDP was to implement the Reintegration Support Scheme (RSS), primarily a mechanism to compensate the 92,000 demobilized soldiers with cash payments for a period of 18 months. This programme was evaluated in 1997 and it was concluded that it contributed to these former soldiers' social and economic integration. The operation, which involved paying the demobilized soldiers, located in various (including remote) parts of the country, was successfully undertaken to the satisfaction of both sides of the conflict, Frelimo and Renamo. It was an outstanding piece of administrative and managerial efficiency. The RSS concept had been put forward by the Netherlands and received immediate support from the government and other donor countries, whose funds were managed by UNDP. Even at the start, however, there was a difference of opinion as to whether the resources (about $35 million) should be utilized to pay off the soldiers directly, or invested in their communities in some way. UNDP could have contributed significantly in exploring creative and sustainable alternatives for the integration and absorption of the demobilized soldiers.

De-mining. The de-mining programme was crucial to reintegration and development. There were several ways in which UNDP was involved, largely through the Accelerated De-mining Programme (ADP) and in managing the Trust Fund associated with it. UNDP played an important role in formulating programmes with the government, providing technical advisors, mobilizing resources, acting as the focal point for external donors, and ensuring accountability and proper management of donor resources. There was a good working relationship with the government, which was executing the programme. One million dollars in seed money for ADP came from UNDP core resources and around $10 million in additional contributions was received from donors. Apart from the ADP, UNDP was also managing other trust funds for de-mining, focused on specific geographical areas. De-mining was an area to which donors gave high priority and resource mobilization was therefore a realistically feasible exercise.

Elections. UNDP assisted the government in organizing national elections. Donor funds for organizing these elections were managed by UNDP. Generally, all parties to the electoral process, as well as the donors were satisfied with UNDP's performance. Election management has been a key area for UNDP in post-conflict situations. Elections are an important ingredient in managing the peace process and also for reintegrating returned refugees and IDPs. Registering people for elections gives them a legitimacy of residence and long-term involvement with their community. In Mozambique, UNDP was primarily concerned with managing the election trust fund and ensuring the administrative and managerial integrity of the electoral process. It could have added more value to its involvement through a more intensive engagement, along with the government and other donors, in examining the long-term capacity requirements, including financial arrangements, for the continuation of the democratic process through the regular holding of elections both centrally and at local levels. An overall and long-term strategy was required for this purpose and had yet to be developed.

Strengthening police capacities. This project, funded by several donors and managed by UNOPS with UNDP support, was a critical intervention in consolidating the peace process. UNDP was managing the programme more in terms of administrative and logistical support and less in terms of making a substantive contribution to the many aspects of policing in a poor developing country. One would recommend a more articulate role for UNDP and its enabling the government and other partners to discuss more intensively the various options and alternatives available. However, UNDP itself did not have in-house capacities for this purpose either in the country office or at headquarters. It was therefore important to consider the development of linkages with other agencies or institutions that could provide the kind of technical support that was required in post-conflict situations.

The Pro-Area Project. The Pro-Area Project in Tete Province was an area-based community development activity, focused on an important province where significant numbers of returned refugees and IDPs had settled. It was expected to be a pilot undertaking that would generate insights into innovative community-based approaches to national development and reintegration. Modelled on the experience of PRODERE in Central America (see page 99), the project had been slow in generating results, although its contribution was considered useful by both the government and UNDP. There were questions raised regarding its cost-effectiveness, particularly in view of its remote location.

As part of the Pro-Area Project, UNDP, in collaboration with ILO, had implemented the Occupational Skills Development (OSD) programme to facilitate the economic reintegration of demobilized soldiers. The evaluation of this programme by ILO had attested to the value of its activities. There were, however, varying views as to its achievements. It was probably useful as a stopgap measure in keeping the ex-soldiers actively involved and providing them with some kind of modest income during an interim period. But there was no evidence that those who were trained secured jobs in the fields in which they learned skills. Training activities were confined to a few tasks (carpentry, bricklaying) and whether there was any value added to this type of training is debatable. GTZ also implemented a project on training, with an important micro-credit component, and it is the view of many observers that linking training with the supply of credit made the GTZ project more successful than the ILO operation. The experience in Mozambique pointed to the need for a more in-depth review of UNDP activities in this area in post-conflict situations.

There appeared to be a trend in community-based area development schemes to follow the PRODERE model, often without proper regard for local conditions. It was not clear why the PRODERE model was considered the ideal prototype. In fact, area-based development schemes should be flexible mechanisms tailored to suit widely varied local circumstances. UNOPS, under a management services agreement, was also managing another area-based project – the PDHL Project – which was funded by the Government of Italy, and which targeted three provinces. It was also following the PRODERE model. Surprisingly, there was hardly any contact between these two projects. In addition, there were other donor-supported projects of a similar area- and community-based type and there was no evidence of any concerted effort to exchange experience and insights.

Resource mobilization. UNDP's experience in mobilizing additional resources in Mozambique had been highly successful. In the last two-to-three years prior to 1999, the level of ODA disbursed averaged nearly $1 billion annually (about 50-60 per cent from bilateral donors, about 30-40 per cent from multilateral financing institutions and about 5-10 per cent from the UN system). While UNDP's own contribution, from its core resources, was a modest $12 million annually, it had mobilized around four to five times that level in non-core resources, tapping into bilateral donor allocations to Mozambique. These had been obtained primarily through contacts with local donor missions in Maputo. As noted above, UNDP managed many trust funds for RSS, elections, de-mining, building police capacities, etc. Donors had been inclined to utilize UNDP as an appropriate and cost-effective partner that could provide services in disbursing their resources.

The relationship between the UNDP country office and local embassies was the key to this type of resource mobilization. This relationship had been managed productively and effectively, although there was a need to re-examine the strategy, which to a large extent was shaped by the immediate needs of the time rather than based on a coherent, long-term relationship framework. Donors also felt that UNDP could make a more substantive contribution to thinking in the areas they were focused upon, especially in governance. UNDP should have considered strengthening the technical capacities of the country office through some additional specialized staffing in its areas of expertise.

III. LESSONS LEARNED

- There is clearly a niche for UNDP in the area of governance in post-conflict situations. Building capacities for improved governance facilitates the reintegration process. The neutrality and objectivity of UNDP is an important factor enabling resource mobilization for work in this area.
- For successful area development schemes to be implemented, there has to be more extensive collaboration with other donors.
- Country office capacities require strengthening to manage the relationship with bilateral donors. Structured systems of consultation and more technical work on the part of UNDP in the areas and issues of interest to the relationship are needed.
- NGOs can be important partners for UNDP in many ways, for example in obtaining insights into and knowledge of local conditions and situations and the practical problems of development management.
- Cooperation with other UN agencies – especially UNHCR – should be further expanded and strengthened such that reintegration projects and programmes can be designed to improve their sustainability, making valuable contribution to the country's long-term development.
- Projects and programmes should not be imported wholesale from other regions. They should be designed and implemented considering the local situation, and with a good understanding of the needs of the target beneficiaries.
- There needs to be increased communication among similar programmes in various regions of the country so that ideas can be exchanged and lessons learned from one another's experience.
- Removing distinctions between IDPs, ex-refugees and demobilized soldiers on the one hand and the rest of the community on the other was a successful reintegration strategy. UNDP needs, therefore, to adjust its overall strategies in post-conflict situations, focusing on regions and communities where these types of vulnerable groups are living instead of the groups themselves.

REPORT ON RWANDA

Training a civilian police force.

The Rwandan tragedy, including the failure of the international community to prevent violence and to protect the victims of genocide, is one of the most disheartening experiences of the last decade.

From 1994 on, UNDP undertook major efforts in supporting the Rwandan government's capacity to design and implement programmes of reintegration and reconstruction, as well as in stimulating and assisting resource mobilization and donor coordination. The Joint Reintegration Programme Unit provides a useful example for practical and constructive inter-agency cooperation which, however, cannot always be taken for granted and needs encouragement, support and enforcement from headquarters and overall UN authorities.

I. CONTEXT AND BACKGROUND

Politically inspired conflict exploiting ethnic differences has had a long history in the central African state of Rwanda. However, in a campaign to eliminate all Tutsis and moderate Hutus, in just three months in early 1994, and as the international community looked on, nearly one million in a country of only eight million people were killed and another two million were forced to flee to eastern Democratic Republic of the Congo (formerly Zaire), Tanzania and Burundi. In addition, large numbers were physically and psychologically afflicted for life through maiming, rape and other trauma. Over the following three years, three million refugees returned to Rwanda, one million of them old case refugees from the 1950s to the 1970s.

The genocide severely disrupted the economy, almost completely crippled the physical infrastructure and deeply strained the social fabric of Rwanda. But in the shadow of this unprecedented and incomprehensible human suffering, the country began to recover. Much progress was made in rebuilding the economy, though Rwanda continued to experience sporadic incidents of violence.

II. UNDP RESPONSE
A. First Phase: Start-up (August 1994 – July 1995)

Redirecting emphasis. UNDP was the first major development partner to return to Rwanda after the new government assumed power in July 1994. During the start-up phase, the UNDP staff concentrated their programme energies on two critical tasks: reformulating the 5th Programme of Cooperation (1993-1996) to address the urgent needs created by the genocide, and preparing for a special Roundtable session to direct international attention to the enormous assistance requirements in Rwanda.

The UNDP country office was authorized, in September 1994, to re-direct programme emphasis from poverty alleviation and development planning to the more basic priorities of helping to restore the State's administrative capacity, re-establish the judicial system and re-integrate refugees and the internally displaced.

Initial funding and disbursement. Temporary UNDP staff was assigned to Rwanda to assist the fledgling government in preparing for the Roundtable to be held in Geneva in January 1995. From all accounts, the Roundtable itself was a dramatic success. However, disbursement was hindered by the lengthy development assistance programming procedures in use among donors. In addition, many of the in-coming officials were unfamiliar with government tasks, and even with Rwanda itself, having lived in exile all or most of their lives.

Even before the delays, UNDP, in November 1995 had tried to remove one possible obstacle to quick disbursement by setting up a UNDP Trust Fund which would provide a means for adapting to the conditions of the country, to lighten the bureaucratic load of donors and to provide for flexible disbursement.

Implementation. UNDP programme implementation unfolded rather unevenly during this first phase of post-conflict assistance. The team that evaluated the 5th country programme during March 1997 praised UNDP for showing institutional flexibility by quickly redirecting programme priorities in September 1995. But the team's report was also critical of the activities implemented under the three components of the redirected 5th programme:

(a) *Restoring State capacity (Capacité de gestion de l'Etat - CAGE).* Although the project "played a positive role in reinforcing capacity of the State in several ministries...it was poorly designed." The number of interventions called for in the project document was too many for the ministries to handle. Insufficient attention was given to the mechanisms to be used in structuring linkages among the ministries. A plan of operation was not drawn up, nor was provision made for a training needs assessment.

(b) *Re-establishing the Judicial System.* Under this component, "beneficial results were obtained which helped in the rehabilitation of the system but there were several serious flaws in the project design." No assessment of the projected needs of the Ministry of Justice was undertaken either before or during the project period. Prison construction was undertaken without the requisite feasibility studies and without any analysis of projected numbers of arrestees, obviously a highly sensitive issue.

(c) *Reintegrating refugees and the displaced.* During this early stage of UNDP assistance to re-integration efforts, the evaluators credited UNDP with helping the government put into place a structure for coordinating and planning, including the Programme Management Unit (PMU) and the Prefectural Support Unit (PSU). At the same time, they pointed out: "it is clear that the structure both at the national and the local levels is quite weak inasmuch as the human resources needed for effective functioning are simply not present."

In assessing UNDP's programming effectiveness in Rwanda during the early post-conflict stage, it is necessary to keep in mind the constraints imposed by the security situation and the political environment. At the same time, however, it is clear that some of the programme's lapses were due to the slowness in response and lack of coordination among international agencies. UNDP, while being pressured by the international community to "do something" immediately, acted slowly since it saw its role, in essence, as that of taking the baton from the humanitarian agencies only when normalcy had been restored. Such a "continuum approach" was based on the assumption that conflict, peace, reintegration and reconstruction followed a linear path of progression, which was often not the case.

Staffing. With increasing international pressure to get involved in the immediate imperatives of Rwanda's "post-conflict" situation, the UNDP country office had to quickly fill Kigali staff needs and often did so with people who had little experience in handling complex emergency situations. International staff were shuttled in and out of Kigali on a temporary basis – including the first two post-conflict resident representatives, each of whom stayed for only a few months. In other country crisis situations, new UNDP staff could often count on experienced and competent local staff for quality support and advice. However, in Kigali during 1994, many local staff had been killed or had fled. Their replacements were mostly inexperienced in programming.

Headquarters bottlenecking. Another factor which inhibited UNDP/Kigali's programme effectiveness was UNDP/New York's relative slowness during 1995 and 1996 in recognizing the need for specially tailored procedures for project formulation, and for the delegation of authority to the country office so that urgent requirements could be addressed in a more timely fashion.

B. Second Phase: Intensive Reintegration Effort (August 1995 – October 1996)

By late 1995, the UNDP office had more long-term staff on the ground and they were working intensively with the young government on two levels. At the national level the government issued the Plan for Reinstallation and Reintegration of Refugees and Formerly Displaced Persons, which was updated in late 1995 with the assistance of UNDP, and was known as "The Accelerated Plan" (PAA). These planning documents tried to anticipate the kinds of support measures that should be in place in the event that a large number of refugees suddenly returned to the country. The estimate at the time was that as many as 5,000 to 10,000 refugees could return each month, once word got around that the first groups of returnees were securely back in Rwanda. During the same period, UNDP launched the UNDP Priority Programme in Support of Resettlement and Reintegration of Rwandan Refugees, aimed at both short-term reinstallation needs and the medium-term challenge of helping to build sustainable livelihoods in resettled areas.

Short-term approaches. Despite the titles of the programme documents drawn up at the time, more attention was being given to the "short-term" than to the coming "mid-term" challenges. This was understandable during 1995 when the feeling was that, because of the enormity of immediate needs, the time was not propitious for designing a comprehensive programme for the socio-economic reintegration of the returnees. By 1996, when considerable progress had been made in addressing immediate needs, it was becoming increasingly clear that the "light" aid coordination mode in effect during the immediate post-genocide stage would have to give way to a more structured coordination approach "to avoid overlapping and ensure complementarity and impact of the various projects underway[12]."

Coordination. The most obvious and talked-about deficiency in the reintegration programmes during the second phase was the "housing issue." Aid agencies were being pushed by the government to build houses for the returnees on a priority basis. In this accelerated drive for housing, insufficient attention was given, in too many of the resettlement schemes, to the immediate, attendant needs of the populations (e.g. water supply, health clinics, primary schooling etc.), or to the creation of sustainable livelihood systems. There was a strong need for better coordination and forethought by the implementing agencies to highlight and address various aspects of a successful resettlement scheme.

In March of 1997, UNDP and UNHCR signed an MoU with two principal objectives:

(a) to reaffirm the commitment of the two agencies to work together in linking relief and development activities; and

(b) to agree to set up a Joint Reintegration Programme Unit (JRPU) to facilitate this operation and the phasing out of UNHCR's reintegration programme in Rwanda. For example, in November 1998, the JRPU undertook a comprehensive analysis of the socio-economic sustainability of resettled groups. By this time, however, more than 40,000 houses for the returnees had been built with financing from UNHCR, UNDP, WFP and others, thereby creating over 140 "new villages." One finding of the survey was: "of major concern now is the socio-economic vitality of these new villages...not all of these communities have been placed in the most optimal strategic locations to ensure...long-term household food security[13]."

NEX Execution. At this time, the modality of national execution (NEX) was proving to be a troublesome programmatic requirement – both for the UNDP staff and those in government who were supposed to do the "executing." The fragility of the state apparatus and the unfamiliarity of government personnel with implementation and monitoring requirements created significant bottlenecks at a time when an all-out effort was needed to accelerate programme delivery. It is true that little real development can take place when adequate attention is not given to reinforcing local capacities. However, during post-conflict situations, NEX may have to be waived until the new government develops implementing capabilities.

DEX Execution. In early 1997, UNDP was preoccupied with the challenge of allocating the increasing amounts accruing in the Trust Fund in the timeliest fashion. By this time, UNDP/New York had come to realize the limitations of the NEX modality in the Rwandan environment and, in February 1997, granted the resident representative the authority to directly execute projects under the UNDP Trust Fund. This decision was crucial as it helped to facilitate UNDP's approval of $23 million worth of Trust Fund programmes over the next ten months.

---

[12] Advisory Note for the 6th Programme, p.5
[13] See "A Study to Evaluate the Socio-economic Sustainability of Resettlement Sites in Order to Define a Plan of Action for the Short, Medium and Long Term."

Roundtable Process. A mid-term review of the January 1995 Roundtable was held in July 1995, and a second roundtable was convened in Geneva in June 1996. The Advisory Note for the 5th Programme pointed out: "In an emergency context it is necessary to ensure that pledged contributions be immediately available.... To this end, it is necessary to go beyond policy dialogue and strategy formulation and ensure that bankable projects are immediately available for submission to donors to translate pledges into disbursements. A greater simplification of thematic and sectoral consultations' format is required to reduce time for their preparations[14]." In general, the question arose as to whether the roundtable was a sufficiently responsive mechanism in the immediate post-conflict period.

C. Third Phase: Massive Refugee Influx (November 1996 – February 1997)

UNDP/World Bank Collaboration. In late 1996, approximately 1.2 million refugees returned to Rwanda over a three-month period. Since neither the volume nor the time frame had been anticipated, *ad hoc* accommodations were put in place for the refugees. A joint GoR/UNDP/World Bank programming mission was quickly carried out resulting, in early 1997, in the government's formulation of a Transitional Programme on Reintegration and Reconstruction (RRTP), which remained the government's guidance framework for all reintegration programmes. It had been expected that the UNDP-World Bank collaboration would lead to a joint harnessing of the institutions' respective programme efforts to improve the effectiveness and impact of implementation. Unfortunately, the desired UNDP-World Bank collaboration did not materialize.

D. Fourth Phase (March 1997 - October 1998)

During 1997, considerable UNDP/Kigali effort went into the design of the Country Cooperation Framework (CCF) for 1998-2000. It contained two streams:

(1) capacity building for good governance; and

(2) reintegration and rehabilitation for sustainable human development and poverty alleviation. A total of $35 million from UNDP core resources had been allocated for this programme. In addition, significant sums from the Trust Fund had been allocated in support of activities identified under the core strategy.

Joint Reintegration Programme Unit (JRPU). In March 1998, the "operational-ized" JRPU drafted a "Reintegration Programme Rwanda - 1998," sponsored by UNDP/ UNHCR/WFP, which called for an investment of $63.4 million. However, the only "new" money generated by this programme was an $8.2 million grant to the Trust Fund by the U.S. In examining the JRPU experiment in Rwanda, it was clear that the concept of a joint unit was an excellent one and that the staff assigned to it went about their tasks in a highly professional manner. It seemed clear that such a joint unit should be an essential element in any "UNDP Model for Post-Conflict Assistance."

---

[14] P. 5, Advisory Note for the 5th Programme

III. LESSONS LEARNED

- Sufficient appreciation has to be inculcated within UNDP/New York for the imperatives of post-conflict assistance to avoid a "business as usual" approach during the early phase of UNDP assistance. Adequate attention must be given to the country office's requirements for:
  (a) qualified and experienced international staff with skills ranging from coordination to activity assessment; and
  (b) the need for specially tailored guidelines for project formulation and the delegation of authority.

- UNDP's traditional "continuum approach" operated by taking over development cooperation activities from humanitarian agencies once peace was restored. However, peace, reintegration, reconstruction and development do not follow a defined, linear path. In post-conflict situations, programmes should be designed and implemented to meet the objectives of all these dimensions, which are closely inter-related.

- Coordination among major assistance players in post-conflict situations is not an issue that should be left entirely to the respective local resident representatives or even their headquarters. The highest authorities within the United Nations organization should play a more forceful role in monitoring and insuring that effective coordination exists among the major UN agencies during post-conflict situations.

- The UN System needs to clarify which of its member agencies have responsibility for managing assistance to various geographic areas or target groups. Failure to do so will perpetuate needless wrangling among agencies, resulting in serious delays in the delivery of assistance to needy populations.

- Establishment of a Trust Fund whose resources are available to all UN agencies will promote coordinated strategies and overcome reluctance to enter into joint programming arrangements.

- A joint programming unit should be set up to mandate programming tasks that the new government is not yet up to handle, slowly devolving these tasks to government agencies as capacities come on stream.

- UNDP should waive NEX requirements in post-conflict situations where government implementation capabilities are weak. While DEX worked well in Rwanda in helping to overcome a temporary implementation bottleneck, it was applied only on a case-by-case basis. When the DEX operating modality is utilized, UNDP should determine whether the case-by-case approval process should be followed, or alternatively, applied across the board.

- UNDP should develop a "special roundtable module" for use in government/ UNDP resource mobilization exercises during post-conflict situations. Preparations should be simplified. Emphasis during the roundtable presentations should be on explaining:
  (a) the need and nature of short-term assistance requirements; and
  (b) how the proposed activities will serve as precursor components for development initiatives.

CATEGORY TWO: COUNTRIES IN WHICH UNDP ACTIVITIES WERE PRIMARILY AREA-BASED

REPORT ON BOSNIA AND HERZEGOVINA

Housing repair, essential for the reintegration of refugees and IDPs.

UNDP could not base its actions in Bosnia and Herzegovina (BiH) on some of its typical advantages, derived from a long, continuing in-country presence. Nevertheless, the organization was able to formulate and implement a meaningful programme of post-conflict support, mainly concentrating on local and regional levels, in co-operation with other donors. In a country where nearly the whole population was affected by the war, it would not have made sense to focus activities solely on so-called "target groups." A number of creative initiatives were developed including the Atlas of Decentralized Cooperation for Human Development, and well-designed, area-based development schemes.

I. CONTEXT AND BACKGROUND

Dissolution of the state of Yugoslavia triggered a war among its constituent republics that started in 1991 and raged for almost four years. The country was rent into five separate states. Following military intervention from the international community, the Dayton Peace Accords of November 1995 negotiated a peace settlement for the region. The Accords laid out, among other things, the basic guidelines for the establishment of peace, the building of the new states and the withdrawal of international troops.

The vast devastation that occurred during the war in Bosnia and Herzegovina (estimated at $40 billion to $50 billion), residual political, ethnic and religious tensions, a shattered economy, continued regional instability and the unfinished task of coping with the return of refugees and IDPs, all combined to produce a staggeringly complex post-conflict canvas demanding innovative approaches and solutions. With refugees, IDPs and demobilized soldiers accounting for nearly two million out of a population of five million, there was no alternative but to address the humanitarian and development concerns of the total population, and not merely to target refugees, IDPs and demobilized soldiers.

An additional twist to the BiH situation was that, geographically, the country is firmly at Europe's doorstep and thus commanded the involvement of the Western-led international aid community. With a large number of UN and non-UN agencies actively engaged in the country, UNDP was a relatively small actor, having established itself in the new state only in 1996.

II. INTERNATIONAL PRESENCE

The Dayton Peace Accords left Bosnia with a highly complex political structure, notably two government entities: the Federation of Bosnia and Herzegovina and the Republika Srpska. There was endemic gridlock at the national level due to the tensions that continued to prevail between these entities. Central government policy making was largely guided by the overriding need for political consolidation and balance of power.

The major international players that assisted BiH in its post-conflict reintegration and reconstruction are outlined below:

Office of the High Representative (OHR): Non-UN international actors played a dominant role in BiH's transition to peace and development. The OHR, which represented the leading nations who negotiated the peace settlement and were active in the humanitarian and development process, was probably the most powerful external entity in BiH. The specific duties of the OHR were set out in a Resolution of the UN Security Council, while the funding and personnel of the OHR were provided by members of the Peace Implementation Council (PIC), representing 50 governments and 20 international organizations. The PIC's mandate was to monitor the implementation of the Dayton Peace Accords, especially the political and civil aspects. There was also a strong international military presence, primarily NATO troops, safeguarding the peace through the Stabilization Force (SFOR).

The **Organization for Security and Cooperation in Europe (OSCE)** was a major presence as well, undertaking many tasks, including the holding of elections.

Special Representative of the Secretary-General (SRSG): An SRSG represented the UN system and headed the UN mission in BiH. By Security Council resolution, the SRSG was also the UN Coordinator in BiH, and was especially charged with marshalling the UN contribution to the implementation of the Dayton Accords. In this capacity, the SRSG oversaw the International Police Task Force (IPTF), with a strong presence of about 2,500 persons monitoring the national police force and facilitating its development as mandated by the Dayton Accords. In addition, the SRSG, as coordinator of UN activities, chaired regular meetings of the UN agencies in BiH.

Office of the UN High Commissioner for Refugees (UNHCR): The most significant UN agency in BiH was UNHCR, with a large staff under its Chief of Mission. Annex 7 of the Dayton Accords recognized UNHCR as being the humanitarian coordinator, and the Secretary-General of the UN had also designated that role to the agency. UNHCR handled not only repatriation and relief for refugees, but also included internally displaced persons in its country mandate. The agency was undertaking a wide range of activities to enable refugees to return and reintegrate themselves.

World Bank: The World Bank was the leading multilateral agency providing development assistance to BiH and also formulated the Emergency Reconstruction Programme for the country. In 1997, it disbursed nearly $200 million and its private sector arm, the International Finance Corporation, also funded several programmes. World Bank programmes were primarily aimed at rehabilitating and reconstructing infrastructure and key institutions. The Bank had implemented programmes for demobilization and reintegration of former soldiers (costing $20 million) and for war victims' rehabilitation (estimated to cost $30 million.) A programme on land mine clearance also had a World Bank contribution of $7.5 million and the Bank managed another $23.5 million of funds from other donors in this area. As these figures indicate, the Bank was a major player in BiH. For this reason, UNHCR had built up a close relationship with the Bank in its operations. The World Bank was also highly influential in the development of macro-economic policy.

International NGOs: International NGOs abounded in BiH, actively implementing programmes of various types. The number of European NGOs operating in BiH was estimated at 180 and the many German NGOs had even formed their own coordinating body in Sarajevo.

European Union (EU) and Bilateral Donors: BiH received a large amount of official development and humanitarian assistance. It is estimated that, during 1995-2000, about $5 billion had been disbursed. EU and most donor countries had significant programmes in BiH. Given the collapse of the administrative systems within the country, donors actively sought the services of other partners, such as NGOs and UN agencies, including UNDP to implement their programmes.

III. UNDP RESPONSE
Selected Typical UNDP Programmes

Five of the larger UNDP-implemented programmes, all financed from bilateral sources, are briefly mentioned here.

Village Employment and Environment Programme (VEEP). This was a programme with a budget of $17.7 million ($13 million, EU; $4 million, Japan; and $700,000, UNDP.) The programme worked with 110 municipalities. The operating modality was to allocate around $100,000 to each municipality to undertake pre-approved tasks (largely the construction and repair of roads and other infrastructure, improvements to water supply, and environmental measures such as reforestation and river cleaning) based on priorities of each municipality. The implementation of these tasks through appropriate procedures was monitored by 50 national UNV municipal monitors. Over 28,000 temporary jobs were created through VEEP, helping ease reintegration frictions. Although demobilized soldiers were given some priority in terms of recruitment for temporary employment, the programme was targeted to the entire war-affected population, including refugees, IDPs and community residents.

The programme was implemented to the satisfaction of the municipalities, as well as to that of the two donors, the EU and Japan. It was directly executed and the administrative logistics, supported by the UNDP country office, had been efficiently carried out. The programme staff was highly motivated and had efficiently undertaken a complex task in a short period of time. While more could probably have been done in terms of dialogue with municipal authorities, continuing interaction between municipalities and the programme made a significant contribution to capacity building.

Integrated Resettlement Programme in Travnik (IRTP). The programme was undertaken with $15.9 million of funding from various donors ($12.5 million, EU; $1.7 million, DBHG {German-Bosnian-Herzegovinian Society}; $1.1 million, UNDP; and $619,000, Japan.) IRTP was aimed at facilitating the reintegration of former refugees or IDP families in Travnik, an ethnically mixed area. The programme was critical, not only for the return of refugees and IDPs, but also for the process of political and social stabilization and normalization in this very important municipality. Based on its success, it was extended to another municipality. Interestingly, a German NGO transferred money to UNDP to implement the resettlement of 70 refugee families in Germany within the framework of the IRTP programme.

IRTP's main component had been the rebuilding of infrastructure and repair of housing, which was successfully achieved. But more important than the physical engineering dimension of resettlement was the highly complex housing politics of the area, with some IDPs occupying houses that belonged to other IDPs and refugees of different ethnicities. Extensive reconciliation of these conflicting claims had to be undertaken before the houses could be reallocated. IRTP facilitated the development of a municipal database for this purpose and also undertook a range of social, legal, economic and civil society activities to enable a comprehensive approach to the reintegration of refugees and IDPs. While seeking to defuse social, ethnic and economic tensions at the micro level, IRTP worked closely and successfully with the municipality towards that end.

Programme for Rehabilitation and Sustainable Social Development (PROGRESS). The programme was funded with $11 million consisting of $6 million from UNDP and $5 million from Japan. PROGRESS was aimed at promoting the social and economic revival of the northwest region of BiH, an area consisting of seven municipalities along the Inter-Entity Boundary Line. The immediate objective was to foster sustainable partnerships among local government authorities, civil society and the private sector. PROGRESS covered a wide range of sectors and issues – infrastructure development, natural resources and environmental management, health and social services, education and culture, and local governance. An important institutional mechanism set up by the programme was the Municipal Development Committee, which established priorities and procedures and facilitated the capacity development of municipal institutions.

About 70-80 per cent of the total resources available to the programme was spent on infrastructure. The Japanese contribution had been disbursed for that purpose in particular. On the other hand, UNDP resources were channelled largely to capacity building. In these seven municipalities, PROGRESS worked closely with the VEEP programme. There was also close cooperation with the so-called "Group of Principals" – OHR, OSCE, SFOR, UNHCR and SRSG – as all of them had many decentralized activities in this region.

Mine Action Programme (MAP). Many donors were involved in establishing the $17 million Trust Fund for MAP. Although its own fund contribution to MAP was relatively small, UNDP managed the MAP Trust Fund. The donors included

Australia, China, Denmark, Ireland, Italy, Japan, the Netherlands, Norway, Sweden and Switzerland. Each donor had its own priorities, accounting procedures and conditions, and there were about 11 separate accounts in the Trust Fund. The government and donors wanted UNDP's close involvement in the MAP. UNDP and the representative of the OHR were co-chairs of the Board of Donors for de-mining. UNHCR made a contribution of over $2 million to the programme, a good example of practical cooperation between the two UN agencies. The programme was nationally executed, with UNOPS as the cooperating agency. At the time of the study, it was estimated that activities managed through the UNDP Trust Fund accounted for about 30 per cent of all de-mining activities in BiH.

The most important achievement of MAP was the development of national de-mining capacities. The programme facilitated the evolution of an effective policy and system to license and monitor other actors. However, there was room for improvement. For example, the programme could have done more to stimulate de-mining operations by other actors, to allocate tasks on the basis of priorities and to accredit NGOs, commercial operators and others in carrying out de-mining.

Atlas of Decentralized Cooperation for Human Development (ATLAS). This had a relatively small budget of less than $1 million, funded primarily through an Italian trust fund managed by UNDP and executed by UNOPS. Many other UN agencies – the former DHA, ILO, UNHCR and WHO – were involved, as well as organizations such as the International Organization for Migration (IOM). The programme's origin was unusual. In the immediate aftermath of the war, many Italian local authorities, civil society organizations and NGOs were extensively involved in BiH rehabilitation activities and had developed a familiarity with local situations. It was felt that this type of inter-country, decentralized cooperation and the bringing together of civil society groups and local authorities could make a contribution in the reconstruction and development phase. The objective was to promote this cooperation and to develop an atlas of the existing connections. ATLAS promoted decentralized cooperation in 22 municipalities in BiH and operated through 29 Italian local committees, which mobilized human and material resources from seven regions, 164 towns and cities and 120 civil society associations. In total, ATLAS was estimated to have mobilized about $9 million from these local communities.

Post-Conflict Concepts and the Bosnian Reality

The post-conflict experience in BiH sheds light on some of the contested issues surrounding relief to development activities. A few of these are described here.

Targeting. For reintegration of refugees, IDPs and demobilized soldiers, the lesson in BiH was that these three categories of persons should not be exclusively targeted for assistance or any other kind of special preference. When their numbers are so large they should be seen as part of total communities and not in isolation. The people who remained in their villages, towns and community had also been equally devastated – if not more so – by the war and their predicaments were as challenging as those of the ones who fled.

It is possible that reintegration can be facilitated through activities directed at specific communities and specific groups. But even more important for effective reintegration are the dynamism and growth of local, regional and national economies. The biggest obstacle to reintegration is the lack of employment opportunities. This being the case, even temporary employment facilitates reintegration and in any reintegration exercise it is therefore essential to seize all opportunities to stimulate both local economies and the national economy. In BiH, the massive flow of resources from donors was an important asset in the reintegration exercise.

Area-based development programmes. Area-based development programmes appear to be one of the more popular methodologies in post-conflict situations. In BiH, there were three or four such programmes in operation funded by UNDP. Often, area-based development followed models developed in other parts of the world (notably, the PRODERE model in Central America.) (see page 99.) It should be noted that we cannot transfer models wholesale from context to context; effective systems of intervention demand that programme activities be designed and adjusted flexibly, with implementation tailored to suit local circumstances.

Sustainability. The concept of sustainability also has to be revisited in the context of post-conflict situations, which obviously are not paradigmatic developmental situations. Nonetheless, in a post-conflict situation such as the one in BiH, a primary requirement is the sustainability of governance and civil society. Even temporary actions such as those UNDP had undertaken (e.g. payments to demobilized soldiers and the creation of temporary employment opportunities) contributed to political and civil society consolidation, and hence to the sustainability of national systems. The concept of sustainability in post-conflict situations must not be viewed narrowly – for example, in terms of the maintenance of a school building, health centre, road or bridge – but in the broader context of building and perpetuating local and national governance systems.

The reintegration gap. In discussions on relief to development and the reintegration gap, the issue of following up on UNHCR activities and taking over from the agency as it winds down its programmes had been an important consideration. UNHCR's strategy seemed to be to ensure that its activities were taken over and sustained over the longer term, and it was working closely with the World Bank and with some other bilateral donors to that end. In BiH, UNHCR appeared to be of the view that what was necessary was an institutional mechanism that coordinated the transfer of activities of concern to it, and to other domestic and external partners. There was a need for a forum to discuss this issue in the context of post-conflict situations at the country level. Such a forum would not focus solely on coordination of humanitarian or development assistance but would deal with reintegration gaps and follow-up of UNHCR activities. The two agencies that could take the lead role in this matter were UNHCR and UNDP, with UNDP facilitating the transfer of functions but not necessarily taking them over.

UNDP's Role in BiH

UNDP came late to Bosnia and Herzegovina – in 1996. By then, agencies such as UNHCR (with its mandate extended to include IDPs) had been on the front lines for some time. Given the magnitude of the international response in BiH, the normal UN system of coordination through the UN RC had been assigned to the SRSG. The traditional role of UNDP had also been further circumscribed by the extensive range of UN and non-UN actors undertaking specific functions such as: organizing elections (OSCE); assisting demobilized soldiers (World Bank); building police force capacities (IPTF); and convening donor conferences (World Bank and EU.) These types of activities were naturally within UNDP's purview in countries like Cambodia and Mozambique, but given the parameters in BiH, UNDP had to seek other critical points of entry for its activities.

Going local. Nevertheless, UNDP established a comparative advantage working at the local level, through municipalities, of which there are about 130 in BiH. In particular, VEEP, directly executed by UNDP and funded by the EU and Japan, established linkages with over 100 municipalities. UNDP was also intensively engaged with municipalities of central BiH through IRPT, again funded mainly by the EU and Japan, and directly executed by UNDP. Through the UNOPS-executed programme, PROGRESS, which was funded by UNDP and Japan, intensive area-based activities had been undertaken in seven municipalities. In the context of tension and stalemate at the central policy-making level, these relationships with municipalities were a critical factor in stimulating local economic development and building social and political stability. These programmes created employment and strengthened local administrative capacities. Also, given the large number of actors in relation to central government activities, UNDP was able to carve out a niche at this key local level that needed to be expanded. The donor community appreciated UNDP's focus on municipalities and, together with other international organizations, was interested in working with UNDP at this level. For example, the military authorities of SFOR worked through UNDP in strengthening municipal capacities in areas where SFOR operated.

UNDP implementation. Another important feature in BiH was that the donor community (or at least some donors) saw UNDP as an implementing agency because they believed that it had expertise and experience in post-conflict assistance. UNDP's core resources over the period of 1996-2000 amounted to only about $20 million, while the funds it obtained from donors through cost-sharing, trust funds and management services agreements amounted to $70 million. UNDP was also directly executing two of the large programmes (VEEP and IRPT.)

Modalities. The whole range of executing and implementing modalities could be observed in BiH. There was direct execution (DEX), national execution (NEX), execution through UNOPS (as well as engaging UNOPS as a co-operating partner), specialized agency execution and execution by a UN Department, the Department of Economic and Social Affairs (DESA). There was also the unusual phenomenon of UNDP implementing a programme for an international (German) NGO. Which of these modalities are to be preferred? There is no easy answer in this type of post-conflict situation. The performance of UN executing agencies had not been consistent and there were many problems, particularly with the specialized agencies. Modalities of executing programmes in post-conflict situations need much further in-depth inquiry. Procedures appeared to be cumbersome and more flexibility was required from all partners. UNDP rules and procedures were still mainly geared to the use of core resources and less to the specific requirements of a post-conflict situation where most of the resources came from other donors.

UNV repatriation. The United Nations Volunteers (which is part of UNDP) played a unique role in BiH. Germany had contributed $1.2 million and Japan another $550,000 to UNV headquarters in Bonn in order to employ about 200 national UNVs who were Bosnian refugees in Germany. They worked in BiH, usually in some UNDP-supported programme. This was undoubtedly only a marginal contribution to the solution of the refugee resettlement and reintegration problem but it had some interesting features. The idea of recruiting these UNVs in Germany and sending them back to their own country was similar to that behind UNDP's Transfer of Knowledge Through Expatriate Nationals (TOKTEN) programme, which sent expatriate professionals who had permanently settled abroad back to their countries of origin for short-term consultancy assignments. A large number of BiH refugees in Europe were professionally and technically qualified and their return was considered especially vital to the economic and social progress of BiH.

Role of the country office. The UNDP country office in BiH was apparently structured to implement direct execution of programmes. In addition to direct execution, the office had to deal with the full range of other execution modalities mentioned above. There was also the relationship with bilateral donors to maintain, which was vital as almost three-quarters of UNDP resources in BiH were obtained from this source. Direct execution of programmes required that the function of technical backstopping be clearly defined and allocated to programme offices and monitored by the UNDP country office. Similarly, there should have been a clearer allocation of administrative and financial management tasks between the country office and programme offices. The country office also needed to be equipped with expertise for resource mobilization, and for interacting at a substantive and technical level with bilateral donor agencies. In addition, the office needed to be more active in its external relations, for example in promoting UNDP in BiH as the international organization with the expertise and track record to work at municipal and local levels.

Information sharing. Apart from random links between programmes and information sharing at the level of a few municipalities, there were hardly any UNDP arrangements or mechanisms for the sharing of experiences, especially when addressing relatively identical issues. The programme in Travnik had little knowledge of what went on in the PROGRESS programme in another part of the country, although there were obvious benefits in learning from other experiences. Additionally, this lack of substantive contact among programmes was not conducive to stimulating more extensive linkages at the municipal level.

IV. LESSONS LEARNED

In many ways BiH was unusual for a country in the post-conflict phase. It was not a very poor country and, as noted earlier, it was part of the European mainstream. It had significant technical capacities and a large cadre of professionals, either within or outside the country. The major organizational structure for post-conflict resolution lay outside the UN system. There were fewer turf battles among organizations and agencies in BiH than in many other countries. One of the reasons for this was that the Dayton Accords clearly detailed and assigned the functions for different agencies. This was also a country where the UN resident coordinator system did not function and the coordination role was undertaken by the SRSG. Although BiH is, to some extent, unique, there are still many lessons to be learned from this experience:

- Economic growth and employment generation hold the key to a successful and effective process of reintegration. Without employment opportunities, inter-ethnic and other tensions mount. Even the generation of employment through temporary schemes is therefore extremely vital to peace and reconciliation.

- Targeting reintegration activities, whether on specific groups or on specific communities, is probably only a limited strategy for effective reintegration. This approach has to be complemented by more general efforts to stimulate growth and employment. Therefore, UN strategies need to be seen as complementary parts of an overall reconstruction and development strategy. In this context, there needs to be a sustained effort to link up with other donor activities, especially with those carried out by organizations like the World Bank.

- UNDP needs to be flexible in its operating modalities. With the field in Sarajevo heavily crowded with other organizations working at the national level, UNDP, by working at the municipal and local levels was able to create an effective niche. Working at the municipal and local levels allowed UNDP to complement the work of other donors and organizations and to create opportunities for an extended range of linkages with donors for resource mobilization and other purposes. Moreover, programme implementation at the municipal and local levels provided the capacity to address an extensive range of practical day to day issues that were vital to consolidating peace and ensuring political and social stability.

- Working at the municipal level required a type of skill and expertise very different from that required for relationships with central agencies of government. Micro issues had to be addressed and politics was very close to every problem. There had to be intense familiarity with the nuances of local society as well. As could be seen in the IRPT programme in Travnik, micro socio-economic problems consumed much time and energy. UNDP staff – national and international – who have worked at these levels should therefore be considered an asset that has to be sustained in one way or another.

■ While UNDP did not have extensive contact with international NGOs at the central level, the organization's programmes established numerous informal linkages with NGOs at the municipal and local levels. There was room for increased engagement between international NGOs and UNDP, which would undoubtedly have enriched the development and reintegration process. On the other hand, UNDP was active and successful in engaging civil society and local NGOs in BiH.

■ The shape and structure of a UNDP country office in post-conflict situations requires more detailed thought and attention. The relationship between the country office and its programme offices should have greater clarity. When the DEX modality of programme implementation is adopted there should be a clear understanding as to who will be undertaking the function of technical backstopping. The country office needs to be equipped with more technical personnel, either continuously or inter-mittently, to monitor projects and programmes. There also has to be a greater country office effort with regard to external relations, particularly with the donor community.

■ Improvements can be effected in the flow of information between and among programmes and with the country office. Arrangements at the time of the study were compartmentalized and there was no sense of an overall, comprehensive strategy by those working for UNDP at various levels and in various units. More avenues for information flows and communication, and also for quick impact training, are required in this type of complex situation.

■ UNDP core resources were deployed for many tasks and for varied reasons in BiH. These interventions were justified on the grounds of their being a catalyst for other funding, seed money, emergency response, etc. There has to be a closer study as to whether these reasons were justified in each and every instance.

■ Obtaining resources from bilateral donors at the country level for organizations such as UNDP should not be too difficult a task, as long as there are clear strategies for utilizing such resources. The BiH experience illustrates the range of opportunities that exist to mobilize resources when significant amounts of funding flow into countries in post-conflict situations. UNDP should maintain a close working relationship with the donor countries, especially at the level of their local embassies.

■ As the ATLAS programme illustrated, much can be achieved by encouraging a decentralized system of cooperation in post-conflict reconstruction by engaging civil society and local authorities to help in the reconstruction and reintegration process.

■ There could be more productive linkages with agencies such as UNHCR and the World Bank. The institutional gap that occurs when UNHCR transfers programmes and function needs to be filled through concerted action by UNHCR and UNDP.

REPORT ON CAMBODIA

The Mine Clearance Training Unit raises awareness of landmines, trains de-miners and carries out mine clearance.

The people of Cambodia went through tremendous hardships before a comprehensive peace settlement was reached at the Paris Conference on Cambodia in October 1990 when repatriation and resettlement of refugees and IDPs was finally possible. The peace settlement included a Declaration on Reconstruction of Cambodia. After a period during which the United Nations assumed transitional authority over key government functions and organized national elections, a new government emerged which took charge of the country's affairs.

Under these circumstances, the UN and UNDP had to face the challenge of creating programmes of rehabilitation and reconstruction and leading them into emerging structures of development and good governance. In spite of a sometimes rather fragile political situation, Cambodia provided a good example of a successful exercise in post-conflict reintegration, especially with regard to the Cambodia Resettlement and Reintegration Programme (CARERE), a UNDP/UNOPS umbrella project. Its contribution to the national SEILA programme to develop a decentralized system for planning, financing and managing the delivery of local services and infrastructure was a hopeful indication of welcome support to an ongoing reform process.

I. CONTEXT AND BACKGROUND

Cambodia had been subject to decades of external war and internal strife even before the fateful coming to power of the Khmer Rouge in 1975, which led to untold millions being killed and hundreds of thousands becoming refugees and internally displaced persons (IDPs). The Khmer Rouge regime refused to accept any assistance from UN agencies. The military overthrow of that regime at the end of 1978 by Viet Nam led to a new wave of over 300,000 refugees who were accommodated in camps along the Thai-Cambodia border. Humanitarian assistance to the refugees was provided by the United Nations Border Relief Operation (UNBRO), which was specifically established for this purpose. The new government in Cambodia did not gain recognition from the United Nations General Assembly and thus UNDP could not establish a full-fledged presence in the country until after another government emerged from an election that was organized by the United Nations Transitional Authority in Cambodia (UNTAC) in 1993.

Indeed, Cambodia was isolated from most of the international community for over a decade. The resulting damage inflicted upon the country's social, political and economic fabric was almost inconceivable. Even after the peace agreement, as the Khmer Rouge boycotted its implementation, reconstruction – always a daunting task – was further complicated for several years by intermittent rebel attacks, causing further displacement and deprivation. The physical and administrative breakdown of national, regional and community infrastructures made resettlement and reintegration initiatives all the more difficult, as did the widespread presence of landmines.

During the 1980s, UNDP provided support to the United Nations Border Relief Operation (UNBRO). Only after the peace settlement reached at the Paris Conference on Cambodia in October 1990 did UNDP begin in-country operations.

II. RESPONSES
UN/government relations

UNTAC, established in early 1992, was temporarily put in charge of control and supervision of key government functions in the country. Under UNTAC's overall responsibility, support for the repatriation and rehabilitation was entrusted to UNHCR and UNDP, which had the required organizational expertise. Thus, from the beginning of large-scale repatriation in 1992, the UN agencies worked without much governmental oversight. This allowed them to operate almost with a free hand but also rendered the quick resolution of some serious problems more difficult. Of particular importance were decisions regarding the reallocation of land and the priorities and ownership of rehabilitation activities. Following the national elections of 1993, which led to the establishment of the Royal Government of Cambodia, UNDP's Cambodia Resettlement and Reintegration Programme (CARERE) project began its reorientation towards institutional strengthening and good governance.

UN coordination

The UN launched a *Consolidated Appeal for Cambodia's Immediate Needs and National Rehabilitation* in May 1992, requesting international support for rehabilitation and reconstruction. A Ministerial Conference followed in June 1992, which garnered $800 million in pledges. At the same time, it was agreed to establish a consultative body, to be called the International Committee on Reconstruction of Cambodia (ICORC), with UNDP providing technical and secretariat support during the transitional period while the World Bank provided the analytic foundation for ICORC meetings.

UNDP assisted the Government of Cambodia in developing its own capacity in aid coordination. The government set up the Council for the Development of Cambodia (CDC) in December 1993 with support from UNDP and the World Bank. The CDC was given the mandate to publish a Development Cooperation Report (with UNDP support) to track development assistance to Cambodia. In all, the donor community provided $2.3 billion in funding between 1992 and 1997, with UN agencies providing $191 million as well as channelling significant bilateral funds (CDC-1998). The UNDP RR/RC held an accepted lead role in support of aid coordination.

III. UNDP RESPONSE

In March 1990, UNDP fielded a mission to assess the needs and possibilities for renewed UN agency involvement in the country. A report was submitted to the Secretary-General that led to the reopening of UN agency offices, to support the Cambodian peace and reconstruction process.

UNDP and UNHCR signed a Memorandum of Understanding (MoU) in January 1991 outlining a joint approach to meeting the resettlement needs of the returnees. Under this agreement, UNHCR was to provide immediate quick impact assistance during the resettlement phase while UNDP, in turn, would concentrate on the longer-term reintegration of returnees and internally displaced persons within rural communities. A Joint Technical Management Committee (JTMC) composed of UNHCR and UNDP was created to monitor implementation. MoU follow-up activities included two missions. The first was a multi-sectoral, interagency mission led by UNDP in 1992. It recommended Rural Integration Strategies (RIS) and provided broad guidelines on longer-term Area Development Schemes (ADS) and a list of Quick Impact Projects (QIPs) totalling some $63 million.

Subsequently, an ADS formulation mission in March 1992 produced the first draft of what later became UNDP's Cambodia Resettlement and Reintegration Programme (CARERE). Based on the mission's recommendations, an advance authorization for CARERE in the amount of $7 million was approved in January 1993. The geographical area of the project included the northwest provinces with the largest concentration of returnees/IDPs and was extended in 1995 to the remote northeast province of Ratanakiri.

UNDP/OPS devised an administrative scheme for project planning and implementation in a participatory framework through Project Support Units (PSU) in four provincial capitals, all reporting to the central project office in Phnom Penh. In mid-1992, the first PSU was created in the Banteay Meanchey province, followed by others in Battambang, Pursat and Siem Reap.

CARERE

Following the model of PRODERE in Central America (see page 99), the CARERE programme was based on the MoU between UNHCR and UNDP, which recognized UNDP's role in reintegration efforts subsequent to repatriation under UNHCR. The central office of CARERE worked under a project manager reporting to the JTMC and the UNDP resident representative. This two-tiered supervision arrangement lasted until 1994, when UNHCR completed its repatriation activities in Cambodia.

Objectives of the programme. The main aims of CARERE were to:
- promote and strengthen the process of peace and the reintegration of displaced populations;
- facilitate quick access by the target communities to basic services, such as health, education, water supply and sanitation;
- promote, over the medium and longer terms, processes of economic reactivation; and
- advance popular participation at the local level for sustainable human development.

In practice, the primary activities of the project included the rehabilitation of secondary and tertiary roads and infrastructure, boosting of agriculture and food production, creation of additional employment, and improvement of the quality of life through health care, education facilities, water supply and sanitation. CARERE began to fund sub-projects from mid-1992. Until the end of 1993, QIPs were implemented for: food production, storage and marketing; potable water supply; development of water resources for domestic consumption and to meet agricultural and livestock production needs; improvement of village level transport; promotion of off-farm and non-farm income generating activities; and strengthening of health and social services. By the end of 1995, the total disbursement was over $15 million, to 475 sub-projects implemented mainly in four priority north-western provinces.

The **modalities of implementation** allowed for diversity in approaches according to the circumstances prevailing in the different geographic areas. While in the early stages, direct implementation by CARERE predominated, over time this gave way to implementation by NGOs, provincial departments, communes, village committees and associations. Project identification was carried out in consultation with the respective provincial authorities and other UN agencies working in the area.

Targeting. The MoU clearly indicated the targeted beneficiaries, which included 377,000 refugees and displaced persons returning from the border camps in Thailand, 180,000 internally displaced persons (IDPs) and about 200,000 military personnel with dependants, who were to be demobilized as part of the Agreement on the Comprehensive Political Settlement on the Cambodian Conflict.

The selection of a community was based on the number of returnees in a particular area. The village and community leaders, in cooperation with CARERE staff, selected the beneficiaries, who almost invariably were returnees or poor families living in close proximity. It appeared, however, that with the withdrawal of UNHCR – which had funded the bulk of CARERE until 1993 – the focus on returnees was no longer emphasized. What eventually followed was a transitional strategy to create local ownership and foster participatory planning in a longer-term development process.

Prioritizing development. From the end of 1993 to mid-1994, a period of uncertainty ensued, partially due to the resumption of low-key conflict in northwestern Cambodia, the decline of donor support and the withdrawal of UNHCR resources. The weak institutional capacities of the local government structures and, more importantly, the problems associated with land distribution also adversely affected the programme.

The various phases of the work plan demonstrated that CARERE also went through a critical reassessment of its role during 1994-95, which led to its redefinition as a project focused on building national capacities for rural development. It was necessary to recast the programme in the long-term UNDP development framework in order to mainstream resettlement and rehabilitation activities. This called for a shifting from relief and emergency oriented priorities to issues such as capacity building and good governance.

Problems. Throughout the period of implementation, the programme faced difficulties of both an internal and external nature. While in some areas, reintegration targets were achieved, in others they were not. The development of local capacity and burden sharing for maintenance of assets remained, in large part, a theoretical exercise due to constraints in generating meaningful local resources. Further, there was uncertainty about continuation of the programme owing both to lagging donor interest and the insecurity arising from the recommencement of conflict between the government and the Khmer Rouge. Other constraints included the lack of institutional clarity on the part of the government, the lack of any legal system, which particularly impacted on the land issue, and the institutional weaknesses of UN agencies and the NGO sector in synchronizing programmes within a broad development framework.

Impact. Despite these shortcomings, CARERE remained the main comprehensive development programme addressing the burden of resettling and rehabilitating a large number of uprooted people whose return, resettlement and reintegration were vital for maintaining peace and stability in Cambodia. CARERE has played a major role in the integration of the returnees by providing a framework of operation and actually managing development in the field. Its dynamic presence also facilitated the involvement of a wide range of NGOs and international organizations in the overall efforts of reintegration.

The Provincial PSUs developed into technical resource offices through which the government and communities could identify, develop, manage, implement and monitor projects. Further, amidst the uncertainties in the political structure and governance of the country, CARERE worked as a catalytic agent, laying down a foundation of cooperation between the government and the communities, and promoting integrated rural development under the preferred principle of community ownership and sustainability. Particular attention had to be focused on maintaining neutrality in a politically fragile scenario with various manipulative actors.

Other UNDP Activities

UNDP developed a Country Cooperation Framework (CCF) for the period 1997-2000. The total core resources for this period were $39.2 million, with non-core commitments of over $50 million. The unusually large amount of non-core resources available underscored the fact that the UNDP programme was seen as a critical response to Cambodia's developmental needs, to which bilateral donors made significant contributions. UNDP also provided $5.8 million from its core funds for mine clearance, human rights, election support and reconciliation.

The major focus of the CCF was Local Socio-Economic Development (LSED), which took up 70 per cent of the allotted resources and included the Cambodia Area Rehabilitation and Regeneration Programme II (CARERE II). Begun in 1996, this second programme reflected a conscious and deliberate move away from the emergency-oriented provisions of CARERE towards a longer-term commitment, covering various schemes ranging from a labour-based rural infrastructure rehabilitation project and support for a micro-finance scheme to assistance for landmine clearance. While CARERE II continued to work in the main war affected provinces, the objectives in the second phase shifted to a focus on decentralized governance and local development incorporating entire territorial administrations and local communities in its support. Nevertheless, with the historic opportunity created by the 1996 peace agreement with the Khmer Rouge and their subsequent collapse in 1998, CARERE II made a major contribution to peace building, reconciliation and the final phase of reintegration of the original target group.

Seila. Concurrent with the signing of the agreement on CARERE II, the Royal Government of Cambodia established the Seila Programme as an experiment in decentralized planning, financing and implementation of local development. (Seila is a Cambodian word meaning "foundation stone.") After four years of operational experience at the local level, it was clear to UNDP/OPS that the prevailing policy vacuum, vertical top-down institutions and attitudes, lack of clarity in institutional mandates, overall weak institutional capacities and absence of any participatory forums were major constraints to sustainable local development. Under government management, and supported by the UNDP Project, CARERE II, the Seila Programme was an ambitious and risky experiment. It aimed to establish horizontal structures at each sub-national level; design new decentralized governance systems for participatory and consultative planning, budgeting, financing and implementation; assign clear functions and responsibilities; and carry out broad capacity building programmes including both formal and learning by doing approaches.

Seila was managed by the national government through the Seila Task Force, chaired by the Minister of Finance with senior officials from the Ministries of Interior, Planning, Rural Development, Agriculture, Women's Affairs and Water Resources serving as members along with a representative from the Council of Administrative Reform. Through the first five-year phase of the programme, a foundation had been lain in half of the country with the adoption of decentralization policies and systems formulated through elected local government councils at the commune level. Seila was firmly based on four cardinal principles for development and good governance: dialogue, clarity, agreement, and respect (for agreements). As such, the Seila initiative aimed at the devolution of authority to the provincial and commune levels through the setting up of a three-tiered system for planning and budgeting (national, provincial and commune).

Under the authority of the national Seila Task Force, responsible for overall management and policy direction, a Provincial Rural Development Committee (PRDC) had been established in each province, chaired by the provincial governor. A significant portion of PRDC programme resources was reserved for allocation to Commune Development Committees (CDCs) for financing the commune development plans. Each CDC consisted of the Commune Chief, an appointed official, and two representatives, a man and a woman, from the Village Development Committees (VDCs). The VDCs were elected in each village within the commune and had 40 per cent of their seats reserved for women by regulation.

The government expanded Seila over time. It spread from the original five provinces to a total of 50% of the provinces and 30% of the communes by the end of the CARERE II Project in 2001. In 2001, Commune Administration and Election Laws were passed that incorporate much of the Seila experience and many Seila design features into long-term national policy and a decentralized regulatory framework to be applied to the whole country from 2002 onwards.

While Seila was a commendable reform scheme, there were still some concerns regarding it:

■ How do the newly created VDCs relate to existing traditional and political structures (village chiefs, elders, religious leaders) and will they ensure an appropriate level of participation in the commune development process?

■ Will a focus on poverty alleviation for the most vulnerable groups in villages be addressed through this framework? As the move into

CARERE II came comparatively early, was there sufficient balance between the emphasis on infrastructure and capacity building on the one hand and the necessary increase in productivity and concern for the poorer sections on the other?

■ Recognizing that the system needed long-term investments from outside, what can be said about sustainability and donor dependency?

De-mining. The Cambodian Mine Action Centre (CMAC) started out as a cell within the Engineers' Headquarters of UNTAC's military component and was conceived as a separate institutional structure that could continue after UNTAC withdrawal. Nevertheless, it was not until 1993 that the Secretary-General asked UNDP to provide technical assistance to CMAC so that it could assume the coordination and planning of mine clearance, post-UNTAC.

A Mine Clearance Training Unit (MCTU) was also established by UNTAC to develop programmes in mine awareness and minefield demarcation, and to train de-miners and carry out mine clearance. MCTU's mandate was extended after UNTAC's withdrawal to allow for institutional consolidation with CMAC. A UN Trust Fund for de-mining in Cambodia was set up in November 1993 and an institutional mechanism was put in place for operations through a UNDP/OPS technical assistance project.

Issues

Staffing. Staffing problems involving quantity and quality affected both UNDP and UNOPS. UNDP staffing was a problem in terms of having adequate numbers of staff with experience in conflict and post-conflict programming. The experience required to transform relief operations into development activities without losing sight of welfare concerns was hard to find. The required system of training staff to work in post-conflict situations was not available in UNDP.

Financial authority at field level. Another problem was the question of how much financial authorizing power could be delegated to the field. For the first several years of CARERE II, every sub-project amounting to over $100,000 had to be approved from New York. The delays caused by this procedure had a detrimental impact on area-based projects that essentially functioned as umbrellas for other local initiatives. Cumbersome headquarters procedures for local contracts and cost sharing also created difficulties and slowdowns. Since 1999, this problem has been ameliorated by incorporating all sub-projects into an annual provincial contract in each of the provinces.

The gap. There does not seem to have been any gap in transition *planning* in the field. However, *programme* gaps did exist, largely due to inherent limitations of the agencies operating in the field. In the first phase of CARERE, it was not possible for UNHCR to maintain assistance beyond a period of two years after repatriation began, nor was it easy for UNDP to target individuals for direct assistance for a long period without addressing key macro questions such as community capacity and sustainability for absorbing resettled populations into an integrated community.

The UNHCR-UNDP MoU signed in January 1991 did not generate the CARERE programme until April 1992, and formal approval for it was not received until 1993. As a result, a time gap did indeed exist between UNHCR repatriation and UNDP reintegration activities. The period 1992-93 was driven by the immediate resettlement needs, essentially reflecting the priorities of UNHCR – short-term, quick benefits directly targeting returnees. UNDP was caught unprepared in mid-stream, due to the shortage of time, the absence of its own resources, a systemic incapacity to respond to emergency situations and the difficulty of overlaying relief-emergency responses upon a development framework.

Turf. It does not seem that there was any competition among the agencies for expanding or protecting their "turf." On the contrary, agencies worked together within their own competencies to reach the goal of rehabilitation in a synergistic, complementary fashion. Nevertheless, different programme cycles and implementation procedures particular to individual organizations did not always aid synchronized action.

Reorientation. During the period of "reorientation" in 1994, capacity building, ownership and sustainability became the primary emphases as opposed to addressing immediate resettlement and returnee needs. While the repatriation relief package, including 400 days of food aid after return, was considered generous, the abrupt diversion of reintegration/rehabilitation resources from targeted groups to the general, mainly poor population was not without negative consequences for the most vulnerable beneficiaries.

Flexibility. There should be a mechanism for introducing adequate flexibility to vary programme modes in accordance with the sensitivities of specific situations. Arguably, the gap would not have occurred at all if the security situation had not deteriorated, if the beneficiaries had not left their places of settlement in a second wave of exodus, and if resources tied to time and donor preference had not been so uncertain. There could nevertheless have been a more serious effort to deviate from the general prescription and to adapt promptly and adequately to the changing situation on the ground.

Given the varying mandates of different agencies working for relief and development, a certain gap in both perceptions and modalities of implementation was sure to arise. No one would question the need to create capacity for sustainability, but perceptions were bound to differ unless a uniform approach to planning, as well as implementation, was agreed upon among different agencies working for rehabilitation and reintegration in the confused post-conflict state of affairs.

IV. LESSONS LEARNED
UNDP Capacity Building

It is clear that UNDP should not engage in humanitarian relief operations, which agencies such as WFP and UNHCR handle better. Still, there is a need and a mandate for UNDP to strengthen the government's emergency response capacity, to create a framework for international co-operation and an umbrella for resource mobilization and co-ordination, and to advocate for a long-term development orientation from the beginning of relief and reintegration programmes. Here, UNDP has a comparative strength because of its continuing presence, acceptance as the UN agency with a generalist development mandate and related holistic view, and established relationships with government and civil society.

Post-conflict Activities and the UNDP Mandate

The need to move away from the perception that programme linkages between emergency, rehabilitation and development are time linkages and the need to situate emergency measures within a broader framework that includes planning and strategy are now generally accepted principles. So too is the realization that development concerns do not cease with the advent of emergencies.

Viewed from this perspective, Cambodia presented an interesting case. In principle, UNDP and the humanitarian relief agencies accepted the need for a joint approach to resettlement and reintegration. However, an initial operational gap on the side of UNDP resulted in shortcomings in addressing the needs of the resettlement operation, which progressed more quickly than anticipated. To respond properly, UNDP would have needed to streamline its procedures at the initial stages.

To improve its effectiveness in post-conflict situations, UNDP needs to:

- Strengthen UNDP country offices to assume post-conflict programme functions. At least one specialist staff member should be attached to the RR's office in such cases. Nationals should be involved in the process from the start to ensure that proposed interventions take into account local conditions and cultural sensitivities.
- Employ appropriate execution arrangements. If national execution is not possible, the options are: OPS, NGO or direct execution. Until now, it was thought that direct execution should only be considered as a measure of last resort. NGOs can often do better at the village level and could be hired under sub-contract. Additionally, if OPS is involved, its office should be present on the spot and report to the RR.
- Understand that personnel involved in post-conflict situations and programmes need different qualifications. Country and emergency experience become more important.
- Re-examine procedures regarding sub-contracts, hiring of staff, etc. in light of the specific requirements.
- Field staff, including RRs, need to be trained to meet the challenges of emergencies, peace building and reintegration.
- Ensure proper co-ordination. It is clear that all parties need to be involved at the planning stage. However, not all country offices will be able to meet such a challenge. Perhaps UNDP could develop a "fire brigade" type of support.

Transition Strategies

Many issues have required concurrent attention during the transition from war to peace in Cambodia. Some of the main points to keep in mind are:

- focusing on the whole community;
- balancing attention towards most vulnerable groups;
- taking into account the special needs of the target groups in terms of trauma, dependency syndrome after long years in camps, lack of (and newly acquired) skills and social needs;

- constant monitoring, using established indicators for the process of integration;
- balancing the social, economic and political goals of rural CARERE-type ADS programmes, which are generally accepted as important instruments of reintegration;
- supporting community participation in planning, implementation and monitoring even at the early stages of an operation;
- understanding institution building as a long-term approach;
- tackling land reform, which has been a central and critical issue for Cambodia for many years and remains largely unresolved; addressing the issue of refugees returning or migrating to urban areas.

REPORT ON CROATIA

Vedran Samunovic/UNDP

Couple returns to badly damaged home.

Croatia, a small post-conflict nation with the main characteristics of an economic and political threshold country, posed challenges to its partners in reconstruction and development that were no less demanding than elsewhere.

While UNDP showed some exemplary initiative in support of area development schemes, observers felt that, in general, a sense of mission was missing and the limited presence of the organization did not allow it to play a meaningful role in the transformation process.

I. CONTEXT AND BACKGROUND

Croatia is one of the richest of the former republics of Yugoslavia, with the most open economy in the region. After declaring independence in 1991, a savage war broke out which lasted until 1995, when Croatia regained Western Slavonia and the southern part of the country. More than a third of Croatia's territory was severely affected by the war, with housing infrastructure and industry damaged or destroyed, agricultural land devastated and livestock killed or taken elsewhere. More than 700,000 people were displaced or became refugees. A significant part of the Serbian minority left the country. At the same time, the nation started introducing systems of parliamentary governance and free enterprise economy.

UN Involvement

On the peacekeeping front, The United Nations Protection Forces (UNPROFOR) and the United Nations Transitional Administration for Eastern Slavonia (UNTAES) held centre stage in Croatia.

On the aid side, UNHCR was, by far, the largest contributor and lead agency. In addition to managing its heavy caseload, it continued to sponsor regular information sharing meetings of the aid community. UNDP worked collaboratively with UNHCR.

II. UNDP INVOLVEMENT

The UNDP office, with a modest staff of three, was opened in Zagreb in April 1996. During 1996-98, about $2.8 million was disbursed out of an allotted $4.8 million.

A first project to support the setting up of a government aid coordination unit was well conceived but turned out to be premature as little funding was available for reconstruction and development.

Area development schemes, established by UNDP, met with considerable success in Sibenik and Western Slavonia, following a participatory approach in planning and local level implementation. The UNDP/UNOPS project in Sibenik provided an excellent example of a well-designed and competently managed scheme of "rehabilitation and sustainable development in war torn areas." Much of its impact was attributable to the leadership of an experienced project manager who made sure that the necessary needs and feasibility assessments were carried out prior to implementation, and that activities were income generating rather than one-time handouts.

In Western Slavonia, too, much goodwill was generated by the UNDP/UNOPS development project. Recognition was particularly due to a dedicated team of national UNVs whose work in establishing local development councils and fostering the participatory process in the area was commendable.

Unfortunately, some of the UNDP projects in Croatia suffered from lengthy delays resulting from the disjunction between field priorities and headquarters response. For example, the timely impact of a pilot credit scheme in Sibenik aimed at allowing displaced farmers to resume productive activities was undermined as UNDP/NY and field staff could not agree on the credit strategy. Headquarters favoured reducing average loan amounts and raising interest rates in order to make the scheme sustainable. The project manager in Croatia argued that there was little demand for the recommended loan amounts and no apetite for an interest rate that would ensure full recovery of costs in the fragile post-conflict phase. When New York finally approved his strategy, the year's agricultural campaign was over and nine months had been lost in planning.

Another credit scheme in Western Slavonia was to have provided funding for savings and loans institutions in order to finance income-generating activities. It had to be aborted, largely because the project design did not sufficiently take into account the existing needs and preferences of the local and national authorities. Again, the level of interest rates seems to have played a role. More care should have been taken to find out what type of credit facility was acceptable under the given circumstances.

An area development scheme planned for Nijemci in Eastern Slavonia was hindered by delays in signing the project document on the part of all parties involved, and by the fact that the envisaged focus area was heavily mined. The site had to be changed to neighbouring municipalities and the work plan redesigned accordingly, which meant further delays and problems.

In December 1998, the Croatian government convened an international aid conference to present its needs for reconstruction assistance and to solicit pledges from the donor community. However the level of pledges (less than \$30 million, some of which had been previously committed) was disappointing, as a real consensus with the international community was obviously not reached.

While UNDP had some successful project activity in Croatia, it seemed that it did not show a clear sense of mission. To a large extent, this lack of clarity could be attributed to its limited presence in the country. More impact could have been achieved if the programme had not been operated almost entirely from New York. Headquarters staff, given their regular responsibilities, could not do justice to the many programming tasks normally handled by country office staff. As a result, the programmes were hampered by lengthy delays, inappropriate project designs and missed opportunities.

III. LESSONS LEARNED

- To make a positive difference in a post-conflict situation, UNDP needs to build strong country staff capacity and allocate sufficient staff for programming and monitoring. Programme design and implementation should give serious consideration to financial resources available for such programmes.
- Adequate priority should be given to de-mining issues, which otherwise can hinder area-based development activities.
- More care needs to be given to the design of credit schemes. UNDP should be ready to modify credit rules during the early phases of post-conflict reintegration so that local beneficiaries can make use of the UNDP credit supply.

REPORT ON EAST TIMOR

Rehabilitation of the Dili-Ainaro-Cassa road.

With funding from Japan, UNDP had been rehabilitating and/or improving drinking water supply and irrigation systems, roads, power stations and ports in East Timor. Implementation was, however, hampered by factors including insufficient consultation with beneficiaries, costs exceeding original estimates and delays in receipt of funds. Questions of sustainability were raised given the lack of local skills, material and financial resources needed to operate and maintain the repaired and improved infrastructure. The following report focuses on a study of the reconstruction activities funded by the Japanese government and is not an exercise in assessing overall reintegration activities and UNDP's role in such activities in East Timor.

I. CONTEXT AND BACKGROUND

Portugal occupied East Timor from the 16th century until October 1975. At that time a coup by East Timorese freedom fighters precipitated a withdrawal by the Portugese Administration. There was then a brief period of strife between

East Timorese factions, followed by a declaration of independence. By early 1976, Indonesia had invaded East Timor and declared it to be a part of its territory, claiming that this was by popular demand. The UN rejected this action and continued to recognize Portugal as the administering power of East Timor as a "non-self governing territory." The Indonesian occupation was heavy-handed and marked by resistance involving East Timorese freedom fighters.

In January 1999, the Indonesian President agreed to let the East Timorese choose between autonomy within Indonesia or transition to independence. In a "popular consultation" on 30 August 1999, organized by the UN, about 99 per cent of eligible voters took part in the ballot and nearly 80 per cent of them voted for independence. The results triggered widespread violence, largely at the hands of pro-Indonesian East Timorese militia. This was brought under control at the end of September by INTERFET, an Australian led multinational force mandated by the UN Security Council.

The two weeks of violence killed and injured a large number of people. About 75 per cent of the population was displaced within East Timor and some 230,000 persons fled to West Timor and nearby islands. Nearly 70 per cent of houses, public buildings, utilities and infrastructure was damaged or destroyed. Government functions ceased with the rapid departure of Indonesian authorities. The agricultural cycle was disrupted, commercial imports stymied, commercial inventories, facilities and equipment ransacked, banks looted, and personal and financial records wrecked. This violence and destruction worsened East Timor's already distressed condition as one of the poorest areas of South East Asia, with 30 per cent of households living below the Indonesian poverty line.

II. RESPONSES

The UN Security Council established the United Nations Transitional Administration in East Timor (UNTAET) on October 25, 1999. Its mandate exceeded that of any pervious UN mission as it had overall responsibility for the administration of East Timor and full legislative and executive authority. It was responsible for security, law and order, the establishment of an effective administration, the provision of services, and the coordination of humanitarian, rehabilitation and development assistance. As of March 2000, a UN force assumed INTERFET's peacekeeping responsibilities.

In December 1999, an UNTAET/East Timorese National Consultative Council (NCC) was established to enable East Timorese to participate in decision-making. In October 2000, a National Council (NC) of 36 East Timorese replaced the NCC. At the end of August 2001, elections were held for the 88 members of the Constituent Assembly, who were to draft a Constitution. The establishment of the East Timor Public Administration (ETPA) and the appointment of the Council of Ministers (East Timorese) in September 2001 followed the election.

The UN launched a humanitarian relief operation in conjunction with INTERFET's intervention. Based on estimates and rapid assessments, a Consolidated Interagency Appeal (CAP) was issued in October 1999 for nearly $200 million to fund 48 emergency and transitional projects through June 2000. With respect to longer term recovery, donor governments, the World Bank, UN Agencies, and

East Timorese representatives meeting in Washington D.C. in September, 1999 agreed to field a Joint Assessment Mission (JAM). The findings of JAM on medium and long-term needs in eight sectors were presented at a conference in Tokyo in December 1999 along with the needs identified in the CAP and budgetary support requirements. About $520 million was pledged for East Timor over three years.

UNDP fielded an Emergency Response Division (ERD) mission in September 1999. An officer-in-charge of UNDP in East Timor was appointed in early October 1999. A UNDP country office was established officially in November 1999. The officer-in-charge was appointed UNDP resident representative (and UN Development Coordinator) in March 2000. In early 2001, UNTAET appointed UNDP as its focal point for capacity building.

Japanese-funded UNDP Projects

Six projects were funded by the Japan Government Emergency Grant to rehabilitate infrastructure for a total of $27,480,000. They comprised:

Dili Water Supply System and Improvement ($11,280,000). The capital city's water and sanitation system was heavily damaged during the crisis. Water facilities, storage tanks, treatment plants, pumps and vehicles were damaged or destroyed. Despite emergency work undertaken after the crisis, the availability and quality of water remained unreliable. The project's objective was to increase access to safe drinking water in Dili and surrounding areas, benefiting some 160,000 persons.

Urgent Rehabilitation of the Dili – Ainaro – Cassa Road ($4,700,000). East Timor's road network had been in a fragile state, largely due to poor maintenance and little upgrading over the years. In the rainy season many roads become impassable, making it impossible for some communities to access markets, schools or health services. The road network was not designed for heavy traffic. After the crisis, the increase of humanitarian and military traffic placed further pressure on the roads. Nearly one third of East Timor's population lived in the districts connected by the Dili-Ainaro-Cassa road, which is the principal north-south road in East Timor. The project's objective was to improve access along this road and thereby benefit some 240,000 people.

Irrigation Rehabilitation Project ($2,737,000). East Timor's irrigation systems were poorly maintained for lack of funds. In 1999, though little damaged in the crisis, many such systems'conditions deteriorated further as some repairs normally carried out in dry seasons were neglected. Functioning irrigation systems were needed to avoid a food crisis and to boost production in agriculture – East Timor's most important sector. The project's objective was to rehabilitate a section of the irrigation system in the Manatuto District and directly or indirectly benefit some 20,000 persons living there.

Rehabilitation of Small Power Stations in Rural Areas ($1,912,000). Of the 58 rural power stations in East Timor, 37 were damaged during the crisis and ceased operations. The project's objective was to repair 13 of these, and help revive the local economy and improve social sector facilities.

Maintaining the Output Capacity of Comoro Power Station ($4,201,000). The

Comoro power station, which was Dili's main source of electricity, was not damaged during the crisis. Power production was, however, insufficient and unreliable because of run-down equipment, lack of spare parts and tools and a shortage of skilled people to manage and maintain the station. The project's objective was to overhaul the generators and provide spare parts to ensure satisfactory production of power for use in and around the capital.

Urgent Rehabilitation Project of Restoration of Navigational Aids and Fender System at the Port of Dili ($2,650,000). Dili's port – one of three in East Timor – sustained little structural damage during the crisis. However, the docking fenders and the navigation aids for entering and leaving the port were in poor condition. The port's low capacity hindered East Timor's economic development. The project's objective was to replace navigational aids and the fender system to enable greater and safer use of the port.

III. OBSERVATIONS
Relevance to Needs
In East Timor the only road linking the capital, Dili, on the northern shore, to Cassa, on the southern shore, was in poor shape, with sections barely passable. Its rehabilitation was highly pertinent to the thousands who lived along the road and needed it for their livelihoods. Similarly, blocked and collapsed irrigation systems jeopardized dozens of communities in what had traditionally been East Timor's most productive agricultural area. While there were more than 50 rural generators in East Timor, at the time of this study, very few of the generators were functional, depriving these areas of electricity for lighting, refrigeration of medicines and foodstuff, and operation of tools and light equipment. In the wake of the UN's entry into East Timor in late 1999, DFID and others were involved in rehabilitating a few of the generators. Electricity for Dili came mainly from five old unreliable generators. The Port of Dili's dilapidated docking and navigation aids hindered current and future sea-borne commerce and services. The stakeholders assigned high levels of pertinence to all of these conditions.

Project Management
In East Timor, a two-committee mechanism was built into the implementation of each of the six projects. The Project Coordination Committee (PCC) included, among others, representatives from ETPA (formerly ETTA), the Government of Japan's (GOJ) Ministry of Foreign Affairs (MOFA) and the heads of UNOPS and UNDP. The Project Working Committee (PWC) included project officer representatives from the various institutions involved in the PCC. In handling projects in East Timor, the two committees were instrumental in obtaining, reviewing and deciding on the pertinent facts; proposing courses of action; and facilitating GoJ/Ministry of Foreign Affairs decision-making in Tokyo to achieve favourable outcomes. The requested seasonal changes to the irrigation project were made in time, before the wet season. Funding for the second phase of the project was approved earlier than expected and as a result, the full benefits

could be counted on. Furthermore, the Government of Japan/Ministry of Foreign Affairs showed appropriate flexibility in transferring savings from both the irrigation project's first phase and the rural power project to the Comoro Power Station rehabilitation project.

In varying degrees all of the projects in East Timor had been problematic to implement, with issues requiring responsiveness, the understanding of all stakeholders, and significant funding decisions from the GoJ. At the Comoro Power Station, the condition of the generators serving Dili was so much worse than originally estimated that, even with additional funding of over $1.1 million, the project was obliged to utilize funds for additional repairs that should have gone towards the purchase of much needed spare parts.

Roles in Project Management

Management of the six projects in East Timor reflected roles that were clearly defined and fully assumed by the parties to the Management Services Agreement: UNTAET and later ETTA, then ETPA with overall responsibility for implementation of the projects; UNOPS for execution; and UNDP for monitoring and ensuring compliance with the MSA. UNDP and UNOPS put into place an effective management structure and, together with local government counterparts and the donor representative, established the two above-mentioned committees that formally involved all the parties to the agreement. UNDP assumed its role fully by participating constructively through the project management mechanisms that it had helped to establish, and by ensuring that it had the technical expertise to backstop and monitor the six projects competently. For this purpose, UNDP built a team of two East Timorese engineers and two international Programme Officers. The initiative had the additional benefit of not diverting UNDP's limited core staff, whose technical skills in any case would not have corresponded to the need.

Coordination and Partnerships

UNDP and JICA collaborated at the design phase of each MSA project. JICA teams, consisting of consultants and JICA headquarters personnel, produced basic design studies, which included the assessment of potential social and economic impacts and institutional capacity of beneficiary institutions, cost estimation and basic project design. UNDP finalized the project document based on the JICA study. This combination of JICA basic design study followed by UNDP project formulation led to the optimal project design and outputs.

The project "Rehabilitation of Small Power Stations in Rural Areas" covered 13 of the 37 rural power stations that were destroyed during the crisis. Portuguese assistance provided through an MSA with UNDP covered four power stations and the balance were covered by the Trust Fund for East Timor implemented by the Asian Development Bank (ADB). Coordination between UNDP and ADB enabled an initial duplication of assistance with regard to a small number of the power stations to be sorted out. The power levels of the generators were standardized. A joint approach was used to address the question of missing distribution lines for the electricity generated and the thorny issues of cost-recovery and maintenance were discussed within the committees concerned.

Timeliness

The project identification, formulation and approval processes moved systematically from the time when the needs were first assessed. However, internal procedural uncertainties at UNDP and preoccupation of staff in the Japanese mission to the UN delayed the request from UNDP for deposit of the GOJ financial contribution. The delay in fund disbursement meant that cost-incurring project activities could not begin on time, and that activities without significant costs but with implied commitments, such as tendering and planning, began with no assurance of when these commitments could be met. Because these activities could be and were undertaken without incurring significant costs, the start-up delay for each project was about one month. Even this delay raised serious concerns among stakeholders, especially the beneficiaries of the Manotuto Irrigation project, as it would jeopardize planting if the projected irrigation works were not finished before the flood season.

Flexibility of Emergency Grant Aid

Because of factors especially related to post-conflict contexts, many of the projects in East Timor faced increases in costs beyond the budgeted amounts. For example, costs of the Comoro Power Station project were affected because initial surveys of the generators very much underestimated the repairs required. Costs of the first phase of the Manatuto Irrigation project were affected by pressure from beneficiaries to change the sequence of repairs between the first, funded phase and the second, as yet unfunded phase. On the other hand, the actual cost of rehabilitating smaller rural power stations came below the projected cost, such that at the end, $478,000 of savings was actually transferred towards rehabilitation of the Comoro power station.

Sustainability

One major risk to sustainability was the shortage of requisite technical and management skills, in terms of both the number of persons and the low level of skills. (Under Indonesian domination, the East Timorese were disproportionately excluded from skilled positions.) The appointment of 11,000 civil servants against some 15,000 approved posts, including the police service and the defence force, has been mainly at the lower levels and less than 50 per cent of top management positions have been filled. Inexperience and the resulting low capacity of those recruited in management positions were sources of deep concern.

The second main reason for potential sustainability problems had to do with the lack of material and financial resources with which to operate and maintain infrastructure facilities and services, including those rehabilitated post-conflict. Physical infrastructure was poorly maintained, and operating and maintenance costs were either borne or heavily subsidized by the State.

Impact

From the viewpoint of affected populations, there can be a long wait between the first contact with international staff assessing requirements for rehabilitation assistance and the actual delivery of assistance. In East Timor, villages without electrical power since September 1999 were first "assessed" with respect to their need for electrical power in late 1999/early 2000 and were still without electrical power in mid 2001. The prospect of more widely available and cleaner water in Dili was also made known at that time, but construction only began in early 2002. Such delays adversely impacted perceptions of international assistance.

Keeping People Informed about Post-Conflict Assistance

Post conflict situations are associated with all types of information: rumours, conjectures, half-truths, first-hand, second-hand, third-hand information, misinformation, and sometimes too, the right information at the right time to the right people. This is understandable given the dynamics at play within and between the national and international communities. Vested interests and agendas of all kinds, concerns over survival and recovery, daily pressures, and hopes for a better future affect the dissemination of information in many different ways. Adding to the confusion, few international staff of aid organizations spoke the local language or languages, and radio and television services were patchy or non-existent.

IV. LESSONS LEARNED

- Projects should be designed with a thorough assessment of the needs of the community. In East Timor, the Japanese-funded infrastructure reconstruction projects were considered highly pertinent by all stake-holders. Well-defined responsibilities and proper coordination among partners are also key to project success.
- Often, even when a project has been well formulated and is on time for launch, delays in project approval and fund disbursement can delay implementation. For projects such as those to rebuild irrigation facili-ties, even a delay of a month can be detrimental, since it jeopardizes the planting cycle.
- In estimating and allocating funds for projects, provisions should be made for unexpected events that might result in increased costs. Tight budgets with no recourse to additional funds might halt project imple-mentation, even when the project is near completion.
- Projects might be implemented successfully but success should also mean that projects are sustainable. In East Timor, the lack of local technical and management expertise and scarce additional funding meant projects could risk failure once the international community left the scene.
- Long intervals between community needs assessment and project implementation can be frustrating to the local communities and can lead to a negative perception of international assistance.

REPORT ON EL SALVADOR

Support for democratic institutions, such as elections, is part of the National Reconstruction Programme.

After more than a decade of intensive civil war in El Salvador, peace accords were signed in 1992, aiming at political reconciliation, reconstruction and democratic reforms. Programmes for reintegration of ex-combatants were of key importance. UNDP's image of impartiality and objectivity allowed it to play a central mediating and facilitating role throughout the peace-building and reintegration process. This position needs to be sustained in conflict and post-conflict stages.

Special programmes were designed in support of demobilized fighters. Reintegration programmes in a variety of fields, ranging from agriculture to scholarships for higher education, were implemented.

I. BACKGROUND

The war in El Salvador began in 1979, in the increasingly divisive Central American political environment of the time. As a direct consequence of the war there were an estimated 100,000 dead, many refugees in Honduras and extensive disruption and destruction in the zones of conflict. Another result of the conflict was the massive exodus of Salvadorans to the United States – nearly 1 million out of a total population of 5 million. (Remittances from overseas have become an important part of the Salvadoran economy.)

By the late 1980s there were increasing efforts to mediate the conflict. The Esuipulas agreements (1987 and 1989) and the International Conference on Central American Refugees (CIREFCA) process helped create space for engagement and dialogue. With increasing recognition that the Salvadoran war was a military stalemate, both sides, weary of war, began making signs that negotiations might be an option.

Peace Accords

After the establishment of the UN Observer Mission to El Salvador (ONUSAL), the peace negotiations culminated in the Chapultepec Peace Accords, signed in Mexico on 16 January 1992, bringing an end to over 12 years of strife in El Salvador. The future of ex-fighters from both sides became the central issue of the peace process.

II. RECONSTRUCTION AND REINTEGRATION

National Reconstruction Programme

Parallel to the Peace Accords, the Government of El Salvador (GoES) had been developing its National Reconstruction Programme (NRP), which received only limited response from donors at the 1991 Consultative Group meeting. The

GoES began to rework the NRP over a period of time, consulting with the World Bank, the Inter-American Development Bank and UN agencies.

UNDP played an important role throughout the Salvadoran peace, reconstruction and reintegration process. Even before the final Peace Accords, it was assisting the peace negotiations and providing support for the preparation of the NRP through an ongoing project and visiting missions. The UNDP participated extensively in the roundtable (Mesas de Concertacion) for defining and articulating the specific activities for the demobilization and reintegration of demobilized soldiers. It coordinated many aspects of the reintegration programme as well. In fact, the Peace Accords indicated an extensive role for the UNDP regarding the NRP. UNDP played a decisive mediating role on several accounts, most notably on the content of the NRP and later between the Secretaria Nacional de Reconstructino (SNR), which was specifically created to implement the NRP, and NGOs associated or sympathetic to the Frente Farabundo Marti par la Liberacion Nacional (FMLN), which had been operating in zones of conflict.

The major problem with the GoES's initial NRP proposal was that it began with a narrow focus. After subsequent revisions, in the final version, the NRP focused on reconstruction support in the 115 municipalities most affected by the war through restoration of services and infrastructure. It had three defined policy areas: support for democratic institutions; support for demobilized ex-combatants, in both emergency (demobilization) and medium-term (reintegration) phases; and poverty alleviation programmes.

A large part of the money administered by the SNR was channelled through the Municipalities in Action Programme. While the decentralizing effect of this strategy was positive, in reality the process was neither democratic nor participatory. In the end the NRP remained a government controlled programme, focusing on infrastructure and only secondly on poverty alleviation.

The treatment of the reintegration of ex-combatants became a major component of the NRP. Yet, it was only in the last quarter of 1992, when encampment of ex-combatants was already underway and the end of the demobilization process in sight, that the GoES and the FMLN reached an agreement on a reinsertion package. The lack of advanced planning on reinsertion and reintegration programming may have had negative consequences on its shape and quality.

Reintegration activities for demobilized soldiers (DS)

After the emergency programme for demobilization (which UNDP coordinated), DS were to choose from one of three options for the medium-term (or reintegration) phase. Each of these three options, or tracks, had specific components:

- **Agriculture:** Household kit, agricultural toolkit, agricultural training, land credit, productive credit and technical assistance.
- **Industry and Services:** Household kit, technical and business training, micro-enterprise credit and technical assistance.
- **Study Scholarships:** Household kit and scholarships.

The UNDP became a *de facto* coordinator of much of the reintegration programme, serving as the major interlocutor with implementing national NGOs. In some instances UNDP even received funds from the GoES to manage projects with national NGO implementers. UNDP managed a number of projects through cost sharing or trust fund arrangements – for agricultural training, housing, and technical assistance for the government or other implementers on land transfer, micro-enterprises, the fund for war disabled and other activities.

Some of the actors involved were clearly faced with dilemmas when putting together some of this programming. On one hand there was a need to remain flexible in the face of an evolving situation and to be responsive to emerging, albeit at times politically motivated, priorities. On the other hand, it was necessary to maintain technical standards and guarantee long-term and sustainable impacts. Improvisation, as was the case with some of the reintegration activities, can often be a recipe for technical contradictions and future problems. There were many compromises in the El Salvadoran context, some of which may not have been in the best interests of the beneficiaries or produced the best possible results.

Agricultural training for ex-combatants was developed as a bridging activity between the demobilization and the medium-term reintegration phases. In the fall of 1992 it became clear that the demobilization process would be delayed and ex-combatants would miss the planting season, and that the process of land transfer would take longer than anticipated. Pressure mounted to rapidly present alternatives for the reinsertion of ex-combatants and thereby avoid the possibility of growing disillusionment. A proposal was made to engage those recently demobilized in an agricultural training project.

There was some debate about whether the project was merely a "quick fix to keep the ex-combatants entertained," but those involved defended it as being technically sound. By UNDP's own admission the programme represented a real challenge to its ability to organize and coordinate such an undertaking. A host of training institutions were sub-contracted and a curriculum rapidly developed. The programme was able to present a curriculum that moved beyond traditional subsistence agriculture, focusing on sustainable practices with a market orientation.

Land Transfer. Although there were enormous delays – due to administrative and legal barriers, the time needed to prepare lists of beneficiaries, and at times, lack of political will – eventually land was distributed to over 35,000 beneficiaries. To accelerate the process land was given *pro indiviso* to groups of beneficiaries. This probably was not a very good idea, as it gave rise to huge problems later on with disputes between beneficiaries, poor use of land and a convoluted, painstaking partition process. The fact that there was insecurity as to the validity of ownership created strong disincentives to work and invest in the land. Much of it was abandoned or exploited in unsustainable, ecologically damaging ways. Another result was that most of the beneficiaries ignored the financial debt incurred and few made payments for the land acquired. As a result, in 1996, by decree, land debts were restructured and the majority of them were relieved. At the same time the need for titling and parcelling of the land was recognized and a project was begun for that purpose.

Another major criticism of the land transfer programme was that much of the land distributed was of poor quality – about 70 per cent was of low or regular productivity. Most of the land of good quality happened to be in high-risk zones, susceptible to floods and drought.

Credit for agricultural production and technical assistance. Land alone does not guarantee that the newly resettled will become effective producers. There were major problems with delays in the acquisition of credit. Also, the receipt of credit was out of step with technical assistance and acquisition of land, and even with the agricultural cycle. Likewise, dispersal of credit was not accompanied by production planning to guide its use. As a result, funds dispersed did not help the beneficiaries attain adequate income levels. By and large those who received credit used the money for subsistence needs.

Micro enterprises. Technical/vocational or business training options, along with credit for starting a small business were provided through a number of implementing agencies. Although beneficiaries in San Salvador performed slightly better, overall the results were poor. Nearly all the businesses had failed and those participating in vocational programmes were not necessarily working in the fields for which they were trained. A number of factors contributed to the bleak performance of this programme:

- the limited absorptive capacity of the market;
- the short duration of the vocational programmes;
- inadequate business skills orientation;
- the young age of most of the beneficiaries; and
- the perception of credit as compensation.

Housing. Recognizing the acute housing problem for those who participated in the land transfer programme, UNDP, with financing from the Nordic countries, launched a programme to provide core housing and latrine facilities. Housing seemed to be a key factor in resettlement as, especially among ex-armed forces beneficiaries, many participants left their lands abandoned until housing was constructed. For many of the DS, resolving the question of housing appeared to be more significant for reintegration than the question of employment. However, much of the assistance in this area came very late, nearly seven years after the Peace Accords. The project was based on a self-construction, mutual assistance methodology, with considerable involvement and contributions by the targeted communities. It had done reasonably well, achieving its initial targets. In some cases, up to 70 per cent of the beneficiaries had already added additions to their core structures. A second phase was added to the project to accommodate an additional 2,000 beneficiaries.

Scholarships were one of the few areas where there was general consensus on success, although a much smaller number of people participated in this track. A total of 1,770 DS from both sides received scholarships for university education, technical training or high school study. Most of the scholarship recipients completed their studies and could expect far better employment prospects than most Salvadorans.

III. LESSONS LEARNED

In El Salvador, UNDP demonstrated clear comparative advantage in areas such as:

- Mobilization of resources and donor coordination;
- Planning, coordination and management of reintegration activities; and
- Mediation between the two parties in order to secure progress on reintegration issues.

However, many activities carried out to respond to immediate needs suffered from technical deficiencies in their design, which limited their efficacy. The reintegration programme for ex-combatants, and the peace process in general, were regarded as concluded by the government. The SNR was closed when its mandate expired in 1996, even though some areas of work were still incomplete. Those who had received land and title, in the absence of adequate technical support and credit programmes were heading down a path of subsistence farming, recreating the long-standing pattern of rural poverty. The most unfortunate aspect of the reintegration programme in El Salvador overall was the extent to which it became a political battleground for the two parties to the peace process.

A number of lessons can be drawn from the Salvadoran experience:

- Benefit tracks should be more flexible. The three-track options were probably too rigid for the reality the DS encountered.
- Training should be performance, not capacity, oriented.
- Reintegration should be demand driven.
- Counselling for realistic expectations and training in decision-making are necessary components.
- Credit programmes should be better targeted and credit not treated as a handout.
- Agricultural interventions require an integrated and synchronized application of different components: training, credit and technical assistance.

It should be noted that legislation for many institutional reforms mandated by the Peace Accords had yet to be passed. Constitutional reforms and human rights agreements had also yet to be ratified. Many thus viewed the Salvadoran peace process as far from concluded.

REPORT ON KOSOVO

Rejuvenating the vineyards in Pec.

Peter Bussian/UNDP

In June 1999, a UN Security Council Resolution placed Kosovo under overall UN authority. The UN Interim Administration in Kosovo (UNMIK) was comprised of four "pillars," each under the responsibility of a different organization: humanitarian affairs (UNHCR), civil administration (UN), reconstruction (EU), and institution building (OSCE). A NATO led "Kosovo Force" (KFOR) provided military security. The UNMIK recovery plan had four broad priorities corresponding to the areas of responsibility for each of the four pillars: emergency and humanitarian support; stabilization of the administration; economic recovery and reconstruction; and establishment of democracy.

With funding from the Government of Japan, UNDP had supported projects to establish independent radio and TV media, supply housing and electrification, and improve schools and education. The following report focuses on the performance of and lessons learned from the Japanese funded reconstruction projects in Kosovo. It is not a study of UNDP's overall role in reintegration activities there.

I. CONTEXT AND BACKGROUND

Tensions between ethnic Serbs and ethnic Albanians over Kosovo have existed for centuries. Since 1913, Kosovo had been a part of Serbia, which in 1945 became one of the six republics of the Socialist Federal Republic of Yugoslavia. Kosovars of Albanian ethnicity, in the majority, resisted what they perceived as repressive Serbian rule from the central Yugoslav government. This changed with the 1974 constitution, which recognized Kosovo as an autonomous province within Serbia. But in the late 1980s a shift in power in Yugoslavia and a rise in Serbian nationalism led to the revocation of the autonomy status. Ethnic Albanian resistance turned violent and increasingly repressive Serbian policies and actions ensued.

In September 1998 the UN Security Council demanded a cease-fire and the start of political dialogue to avoid an impending human catastrophe in Kosovo. The violence continued, prompting a March 1999 air campaign, which the North Atlantic Treaty Organization (NATO) carried out against Serbian forces in Kosovo to exert pressure on the Yugoslav leadership, which by then was pursuing a policy of driving Kosovar Albanians from their homes. The air campaign ended in June 1999, after Yugoslavia's leadership agreed to a set of conditions and pulled its forces out of Kosovo, and NATO "Kosovo Force" (KFOR) troops occupied the entire province soon after.

There were large numbers of persons killed and injured in the conflict between March and June 1999, as well as major population displacements. Of Kosovo's pre-conflict population of some two million, which was 80 per cent to 90 per cent ethnic Albanian, some 800,000 people, including around 100,000 Serbian Kosovars, left the province. Another 500,000 were internally displaced. Housing and public buildings were extensively damaged and all commercial, agricultural and public service activities severely disrupted. The consequences of the conflict exacerbated pre-existing difficulties. Kosovo had one of the region's poorest economies, with high unemployment, low productivity, lack of investment and deteriorated infrastructure. It had experienced communist systems of planning and social ownership, characterized by a lack of transparency and accountability. In the 10 years that preceded the conflict, most Kosovars of non-Serb ethnicity were removed from or felt compelled to leave responsible positions, resulting in an ethnic Albanian work force of limited technical and management ability.

II. RESPONSES

In June 1999, a UN Security Council Resolution placed Kosovo under overall UN authority. The UN Interim Administration in Kosovo (UNMIK) was comprised of four "pillars," each under the responsibility of a different organization:

humanitarian affairs (UNHCR), civil administration (UN), reconstruction (EU) and institution building (OSCE). A NATO led "Kosovo Force" (KFOR) provided military security. The UNMIK recovery plan had four broad priorities corresponding to the areas of responsibility or each of the four pillars: emergency and humanitarian support; stabilization of the administration; economic recovery and reconstruction; and establishment of democracy.

A UNDP office was established in August 1999 and a UNDP resident representative, appointed in October of that year, was also designated UN Development Coordinator in March 2000. In March 2000 the Government of Japan also established a small office in Pristina, staffed by personnel who were being rotated from its office in Belgrade.

UNDP Projects (funded by the Government of Japan)

Support to Kosovo Independent Media (KIM) Project ($14,500,000). After the revocation of Kosovo's autonomy in 1984, the media and public information system were put under state control and staffed essentially by ethnic Serbs. These information services were politicized and failed to meet democratic standards either professionally or ethically. Television and radio facilities – both studio and transmission equipment – were old, in poor condition and had been partly damaged or destroyed during the 1999 conflict.

The OSCE (within UNMIK, in charge of institution building and media development in Kosovo) approached the Government of Japan through UNDP/UNOPS in late 1999 for support in developing Radio Television Kosovo (RTK) as an independent public media organization. Further discussions among the Government of Japan, the OSCE, UNDP and UNOPS led to agreement in May 2000 on a project with three components: a terrestrial transmission system; radio and television studio equipment; and a radio and television production training facility.

Housing and Electrification in Kosovo ($19,998,000). The overall housing needs were first presented at a donor conference in Brussels in July 1999. The Japanese mission that visited Kosovo in August reviewed them further and discussed possible funding for reconstruction with the EU (within UNMIK responsible for reconstruction), UNDP and UNOPS. An electrification component was added subsequently (see below) and the project's overall title became "Housing and Electrification in Kosovo (HEIK)." UNDP and UNOPS fielded an initial project formulation mission in October 1999.

The project was revised during the following year to reflect changes in funding and implementation modalities. In its final form, the project's objective was to reconstruct 700 - 1,000 rural dwellings in the Peja, Skenderaj and Rehovec districts. It also aimed to provide technical and managerial training to the communities involved.

Electrification Component. Kosovo's electricity system had consisted of three generating stations; power connections from Albania, Macedonia, Montenegro and Serbia for the import of some power; transmission lines; and seven electricity distribution centres. The system had an average age of nearly 40 years and was inefficient and generally unreliable. Technicians and managers were too few, and poorly trained and equipped. The transmission and distribution systems were severely damaged during the conflict and thousands of homes were left without electricity as a result.

The electrification component was added to the housing component during the formulation mission for the HEIK project in October 1999. Objectives were to rehabilitate part of the electrification sector in the areas of Mitrovice and Skenderaj, benefiting some 4,000 customers; and to provide technical and managerial training to the communities involved.

Social Rehabilitation in Kosovo ($2,700,000). Education was a highly solicited sector, as half of the population of Kosovo was under the age of 20. Since the summer of 1999, some 28,000 educational staff and 400,000 students had re-entered the education system at primary, secondary and tertiary levels. The conflict severely affected the sector, partly because of the considerable damage to and looting of school facilities, teaching aids and furnishings. In 1998 there were 1,200 school buildings in Kosovo; some 800 of these were destroyed or severely damaged.

UNDP undertook project formulation in mid-2000 in consultation with the Government of Japan, UNMIK and international organizations active in the education sector. The project aimed to improve school conditions and create safer learning environments for students at three primary schools and two high schools in the Prizran Region, thus benefiting some 2,500 students.

III. OBSERVATIONS
Relevance of the Assistance

The KIM project in Kosovo addressed the clear need for balanced, informative radio and television broadcasts that were culturally relevant to the entire population. With regard to the HEIK project, on-site visits quickly confirmed statistics on the destruction of housing, as well as information on the rudimentary living conditions of impoverished families. Also evident was the need for electricity and the insufficiency of means for producing and distributing it. The evaluation team saw firsthand the inadequate learning environments of several hundred pupils crowded into what remained of two schools and could attest to the pertinence of reconstructing these facilities.

The Kosovo projects provided homes for a thousand families, reliable electric power for dozens of communities and a better learning environment for several thousand students. If successful, the infrastructure projects could contribute significantly to human security, development and poverty eradication among populations that had long been, and still were, the poorest in their geographical regions. While short-term success was likely (i.e. physical infrastructure successfully rehabilitated), longer-term success necessary to meet goals for human security, development and poverty reduction appeared problematic, given the paucity of financial, material and human resources to manage, maintain and operate the infrastructure. These factors appeared not to have been sufficiently recognized. All of the infrastructure projects were "entry points" for policy advice, institution building and governance initiatives at various levels, and in various sectors.

Project Management

The progress and results of a project greatly depend on how it is managed. In post-conflict contexts, effective project management requires taking into account the inherent uncertainties, the number of actors, their differences and the complexity of relationships and constraints in logistics and communications. In Kosovo, a UNOPS Project Management Unit (PMU) based in Pristina implemented the HEIK project, separated into components for housing and electricity. The PMU was also to have implemented the KIM project, but it was implemented by UNOPS staff in New York and Geneva who periodically travelled to Kosovo, supported by UNDP staff in Pristina. The education project was to be implemented by an NGO using its own project-management mechanism.

Roles in Project Management

The KIM project placed sizeable demands on UNDP staff, who had to carry out effective backstopping and monitoring of multi-million dollar rehabilitation projects in Kosovo. Even if project management units or facilities have been established to implement projects, knowledgeable staff must be sufficiently available.

Coordination and Partnerships

Generally, the various arrangements for the coordination of international assistance had been sufficient to ensure that there was no duplication between the assistance provided through the projects and those of other donors. In Kosovo, however, in the project "Support to Kosovo Independent Media," the component for the establishment of the terrestrial broadcasting system suffered the adverse consequences of an insufficient and delayed framework for coordination. In this case, the Government of Japan/UNDP project and comparable USAID assistance progressed on similar tracks, ostensibly without the parties concerned knowing of each other's activities. This was in spite of the fact that the OSCE had overall executing responsibility for the project and, in addition, had the lead role for media affairs within UNMIK. A collaborative framework was eventually developed after a series of painful negotiations.

Timeliness

The start of the HEIK project in Kosovo was slowed significantly by difficulties in obtaining project approvals and/or releases of funds. The KIM project was in turn hindered by the late start of the HEIK project, as the PMU planned for the HEIK project was also to have covered the KIM project but was not operational until six months after that project began.

Flexibility of Emergency Grant Aid

Virtually all projects in Kosovo faced, or were likely to face, increases in costs beyond the budgeted amounts. For example, costs of materials and transport in Kosovo had risen some 10 per cent beyond those used to calculate the budget approved for the HEIK project. Costs for the KIM project were likely to increase significantly due to the equipment changes needed because of retransmission locations and output levels different from those already agreed upon.

While solutions must be found to such changed costs, they were generally made through budgetary reallocations that sometimes involved reducing quality (e.g. in HEIK, substituting wooden for concrete electricity poles; or in the KIM project, suspending an activity such as training.)

Sustainability

Most of the projects in Kosovo were likely to face severe to moderate sustainability problems. In some cases, project benefits would be greatly diminished unless sustainability could be assured. One major risk was the shortage of requisite technical and management skills, in terms of both the number of persons and the level of skills. In Kosovos's final decade of Serbian domination, the now dominant Albanian population was excluded from positions where its members could have acquired or exercised such skills.

Another factor limiting development of skills in the target population was that training in the infrastructure projects largely consisted of on-the-job experience that was mainly technical, and directly associated with project implementation. Donor grants typically provided only for training strictly necessary to furnish the specified assistance. This contrasts with other types of grant aid, such as project-type technical cooperation that combines grant aid with technical assistance.

The second main reason for potential sustainability problems had to do with the lack of material and financial means with which to operate and maintain infrastructure facilities and services. Physical infrastructure was poorly maintained in Kosovo and, in some cases, destroyed in the conflicts while associated materials, machinery and parts were looted. Operating costs were borne by the State, or if paid by the beneficiaries, heavily subsidized. The sizes of the pre-conflict and post-conflict government bureaucracies were disproportionately large in relation to the sizes of the respective populations and economies.

Impact

From the viewpoint of affected populations, there can be a long wait between the first contact with international staff assessing requirements for rehabilitation assistance and the actual delivery of assistance. In Kosovo, over a year passed, including two winters, for most beneficiaries between the time consultations were held and work actually started on reconstruction. This resulted in creating negative impressions about international assistance.

Keeping People Informed About Post-Conflict Assistance

Post-conflict situations come with all types of information, from fabricated rumours to the right information at the right time. This is understandable, given the dynamics at play within and between the national and international communities. Interests and agencies of all kinds, concerns over survival and recovery, daily pressures, and hopes for a better future affect the dissemination of information in many different ways. Adding to the confusion, few international staff of aid organizations are likely to speak the local language or languages and radio and television services may be patchy or non-existent. The situation in Kosovo fitted this norm. Thus, for post-conflict assistance in general, and for the projects under review in particular, there was a need for sustained and proactive efforts to keep stakeholders, beneficiaries, and the general public informed, in appropriate detail, of intentions, commitments and progress with respect to the assistance planned or being provided.

Visibility is also important. In Kosovo, where international donors and organizations readily publicized their work, numerous signs and stickers attested to the Government of Japan/UNDP partnership in the HEIK and KIM projects.

IV. LESSONS LEARNED

- While projects and programmes might be highly relevant and considered successful in the short-term (i.e. physical infrastructure successfully rehabilitated), longer-term success necessary to meet goals for human security, development and poverty reduction cannot be assured in an environment where the financial, material and human resources needed to manage, maintain and operate the infrastructures are lacking. These issues seemed to be recognized and addressed in the case of Kosovo.

- In post-conflict situations, early availability of qualified personnel, funds and equipment are critical requirements if UNDP is to meet its responsibilities in large post-conflict projects, and this should not be met by diverting staff from core functions of the country office.

- Delays in project approval and fund disbursement not only interrupt a project's schedule and timely deliverance but lead to wasteful cost increases. Often, this can be a frustrating experience for the organizations and people involved in making projects and programmes successful.

- Development projects and programmes should factor in unexpected circumstances and make room for contingencies so as to provide emergency funding flexibility to meet such demands.

- Local capacities need to be developed to manage and maintain infrastructure projects. Adequate hiring and training of local personnel is important in infrastructure reconstruction.

REPORT ON THE PHILIPPINES

Seaweed production provides livelihoods.

The peace agreement between the Government of the Philippines and the Moro National Liberation Front (MNLF) was initially implemented with some success in turning communities of fighters into production-oriented villages. However the peace process then faced a crisis of credibility as little progress was made on the issues of effective autonomy and increased investment – key areas of government commitment.

In cooperation with the government, UNDP carved out a multi-donor programme, winning the support of bilateral donors and UN agencies as well as the confidence of the MNLF. Thus, the UN group played an important and recognized role in sustaining peace in Mindanao.

I. CONTEXT AND BACKGROUND

Despite self-rule and the independence of the Philippines as a republic in 1945, governmental policies perpetuated the social, economic and political marginalization of the predominantly Muslim populations who lived in the southern Philippines (Mindanao). The indigenous people began to call for independence and organized armed conflict, which intensified under the 20-year Marcos military dictatorship.

In September 1996, the Government of the Republic of the Philippines and the Moro National Liberation Front (MNLF) entered into a Peace Agreement that put an end to more than two decades of armed conflict between them in the southern Philippines. The Agreement was brokered by the Organization of the Islamic Conference (OIC), which extended its assistance and good offices to monitor the implementation during the transitional period of three years.

The first Organization of the Islamic Conference (OIC) brokered peace agreement was signed in 1976 in Tripoli, and, among other things, provided for limited autonomy in 13 provinces in the southern Philippines. It failed mainly because it was not sufficiently implemented. Little progress was made until the restoration of democracy in 1986, after which peace negotiations were again pursued at various fronts with the major rebel groups, including the MNLF. In 1989, the Autonomous Region of Muslim Mindanao (ARMM) was established. While a step in the right direction, it was considered insufficient in terms of a solution to the conflict in Mindanao. The rebellion then splintered and new factions emerged from ideological and leadership differences, including the Moro Islamic Liberation Front (MILF) and the Abu Sayyaf groups. The (communist-oriented) National People's Army also operated in the southern Philippines, capitalizing on the lack of opportunities for the indigenous population within an economically growing region.

The Peace Agreement and its Implementation

The 1996 Agreement was concluded only with the MNLF, the largest of the resistance groups. The MILF, Abu Sayyaf and the NPA remained active, though with limited support. However, as the first three-year phase drew to an end, disillusionment with perceived inadequate response by the government resulted in the defection of some MNLF members to the MILF, which continued to engage in armed warfare with both government troops and the MNLF. Early in 1999, a tentative cease-fire was reached with the MILF, followed by negotiations which, had they been successful, could have widened the opportunity for peace and confidence building measures. Instead, further confrontation and military intervention followed.

The three-year transitional period included the establishment of a Special Zone of Peace and Development (SZOPAD) covering 14 provinces and nine cities, and the creation of a Southern Philippines Council for Peace and Development (SPCPD) to promote and coordinate development efforts in the special zone. A limited number of MNLF fighters were to join the national security forces. A peculiar feature of the Agreement was that the main MNLF forces were not disarmed, maintaining the military command structure while the ex-combatants lived in "camps" with their families. While this may have sustained the potential for renewed violence, it also offered a chance to involve whole units in the reintegration process as the camps moved to villages and engaged in cooperative community development.

Observers spoke of a historic opportunity for peace, built upon the two key pillars of autonomy and development support. Unfortunately, the "Mini-Marshall Plan" envisaged by the Ramos administration did not materialize and, as no increase in public funding and investment occurred in the region, its leaders complained of the missing additionality of the expected peace dividend. One reason for the government's failure to deliver as per its commitment was the onslaught of the South East Asian economic crisis. Whatever the reasons, the lack of response from the government seriously hindered and undermined the intended peace process, as well as the position of its proponents.

As it turned out, external assistance became all the more important, as it was practically the only additional input available at the time. On the other hand, the international community could not possibly meet all the high expectations and related promises arising from the Peace Agreement. In spite of efforts to join hands in a major programme of assistance, international donors were only partly able to meet the challenge. Nor were they able to avoid the resulting crisis of credibility and growing frustration that eventually led to renewed violence and confrontation.

II. UNDP RESPONSE

Following the Peace Agreement, the United Nations, hoping to assist in cementing the fragile peace, began discussing possibilities for an UN/multi-donor assistance package for the socio-economic reintegration of the MNLF ex-combatants. The initiative was favourably supported and at the specific request of the government, the UN system under the leadership of the RC developed a "UN Expanded Programme of Assistance for Delivery of Basic Services, Livelihood Development, Enterprise and Skills Development, and Capacity Building for MNLF Soldiers, their Families and their Communities." FAO, ILO, UNDP, UNFPA and UNICEF were partners in its implementation, with the SPCPD. Bilateral donors included Australia, Belgium, Canada, Netherlands, New Zealand, Norway, Spain, Sweden and Switzerland.

The first phase of preparatory work started in early 1997, including a needs assessment exercise and pilot-test of relief and rehabilitation assistance. This approach was useful inasmuch as it involved MNLF leaders and selected communities, and resulted in the collection of information about their reintegration requirements. But it also caused additional delays in programming UN cooperation at a time when some major bilateral donors had already established their presence on the ground and were delivering assistance.

The information garnered in the needs assessment became the basis for the formulation of activities for the second phase, a multi-agency effort consisting of five programme components with activities in 16 provinces, which began in April 1998. Six organizations (FAO, ILO, IOM, UNDP, UNFPA and UNICEF) agreed in principle to assume responsibility for the execution of the different programme components. These were in the following areas: delivery of basic services (health, water and sanitation, primary education); agricultural livelihoods; vocational skills training and enterprise/cooperative management; human resources development (leadership and governance training for MNLF and SPCPD members); and mobile information, referral and community assistance services.

The second phase was formulated to provide an expanded package of assistance directed towards meeting basic needs and enhancing the opportunities for the reintegration of MNLF soldiers into mainstream economy and society. More specifically, the second phase was targeted at:[15]

- Providing the MNLF and family units with gainful employment and income through agricultural livelihood opportunities, enterprise development and skills training;
- Improving the living conditions in target communities through emergency assistance and delivery of basic services;
- Transforming MNLF politico-military structures into viable civilian development organizations capable of mobilizing resources for the delivery of basic services and livelihood assistance to their members;
- Building the capacity of MNLF leaders as development catalysts and managers;
- Building the capacity of the SPCPD secretariat for effective coordination of development initiatives; and
- Fostering confidence building among MNLF communities, the government and civil society at large towards long-term development partnerships.

---

[15] Pilot Country Level Impact Assessment (CLIA) report on Philippines, draft April 2002

III. OBSERVATIONS
UN Action: Joint Programme Framework for Project Delivery

At the 1996 Consultative Group meeting in Tokyo, donor and government representatives called for "joint programming exercises" in Mindanao. Subsequently, the Resident Coordinator met with the Government of the Philippines to discuss the possibility of developing a UN Programme for Peace and Development in Mindanao. This coincided with the UN Development Assistance Framework (UNDAF) process in the Philippines. Thus, the development of a timely response to the post-Peace Agreement needs of the MNLF created an opportunity to put a coordinated UN programme into practice. At the same time, it demonstrated that the UN could respond to the post-conflict needs of a minority area in the country.

A process of discussion followed. Many donors found the UN system's approach attractive and were ready to support it. However, despite the interest in and commitment to having a joint UN programme, there were difficulties in identifying mechanisms for transferring funds from a UNDP trust fund to other agencies. Despite the fact that both the donors and the RC would have preferred to have a joint UN programme, there was no legal framework in which the UNRC office could bring activities together (except for the UNDP cost sharing arrangement, which was not acceptable to all UN agencies.) The result was an array of projects within one common programme framework.

The UNDP and the office of the RC worked hard to pursue a UN system effort through a programme approach engaging a whole group of UN agencies. Despite rules and regulations, which often presented serious obstacles to constructive interventions in the post-Peace Agreement environment, UNDP was persistent in trying to get things moving, although it was not always possible to get the full participation and coordination of the agencies.

There were complaints from UNDP, SPCPD and MNLF regarding the cumbersome and centralized procurement procedures of the UN system, which led to unnecessary delays in project implementation. Obviously, delays in post-conflict project implementation have significant political impact. The experience of procurement procedures driving programme design points to an institutional problem that the UN system has in responding with agility and effectiveness in post-conflict situations. The UNDP country office had recommended that it be given authority for field office procurement and implementation, on a case by case basis, to speed up implementation.

Peace-building Impact: Effective Peace and Development Approach

The MNLF, government, donors and UN agencies affirmed the positive impact of the programme in maintaining the fragile peace. There were tensions between the MNLF and the government, with the MILF trying to win over the discontented MNLF fighters and return them to armed combat. Therefore, the programme was critical in demonstrating that the SPCPD could deliver. The fact that the UN used SPCPD as the executing agency, with FAO, ILO and UNDP support in implementation, strengthened SPCPD and MNLF organizational skills. It also brought the MNLF into the details of project implementation so that members understood project parameters and limitations, which helped to bring expectations to more realistic levels.

There was no doubt that the programme and the overall actions of the UN system had a positive contribution to peace in Mindanao. This probably was the real value of this undertaking – its contribution to the consolidation of peace through confidence building, which was breaking down the walls and mistrust that existed between Muslim and Christian communities, and between the MNLF and the government.

Perhaps more could have been done in the area of peace promotion. There was a need to promote dialogue and understanding between Muslim and non-Muslim communities to cultivate relationships and break down the entrenched mistrust. It must also be added that there was a widely held belief among the MNLF that the peace-building and development programmes in Mindanao were donors' programmes implemented under the leadership of the UN and not government programmes.

Skills and Capacity Building to Move the MNLF from a Military Force to a Development Organization

In other countries, a common component of a peace process has been the transformation of an armed opposition into a political party with legal status. In the Philippines, the process had to be somewhat different. In the regional, ethnic conflict, the MNLF did not appear to have national political aspirations and the creation of a political party had not been a priority. Rather, the transformation of the military structure had been focused on the creation of localized developmental organizations.

Skills training and capacity building were the key issues. For the most part, most MNLF supporters and militants lacked education and practical experience in administration, management and development issues. This was a major hindrance to the effectiveness of the SPCPD and the new economic ventures. It also made it difficult for the UN to achieve, in staff recruitment, some kind of a balance between the different groups of the population, an issue of much discussion and some complaint by local leaders.

Apart from the upgrading of the professional performance of MNLF members within the SPCPD, the main strategy pursued was the transformation of the MNLF's structures into multi-purpose cooperatives. The programme supported this process and these cooperatives were the principal target groups and beneficiaries. The strategy was to build a sustainable development organization within the MNLF community while strengthening the experience and capacity of its members at the same time. Training was provided and linkages with educational centres established to guide the transformation process.

Occasionally, critical questions were raised as to whether it was justified to concentrate emphasis and resources on a temporary structure with a limited mandate like the SPCPD, whose future was seen as uncertain. However, there was no viable alternative, and the participation of many MNLF leaders in the SPCPD helped achieve a considerable amount in terms of capacity building, which could carry over into future arrangements. In fact, some of the MNLF leaders had already been elected to offices in the local administration.

In view of the limited job opportunities, not all the skills training led to subsequent employment. Though this was perhaps a common feature of many similar programmes, it needs special attention when dealing with a group of people expecting to start a new life after years of hardship and sacrifice.

There was some resentment among non-MNLF community members since the programmes targeted only MNLF members when they were just one part of the Mindanao community. A more holistic programme targeting the entire community would have been more appreciated and led to increased community participation. On the other hand, given limited resources and the priorities of bringing the MNLF soldiers into the development fold, there were few alternatives but to focus on the MNLF members.

Support for Livelihoods

Most of the training, agricultural, livelihood and other projects supported by the programme were implemented through the state multi-purpose cooperatives. In some cases, smaller subsidiary cooperatives were established in the municipalities of a state. The envisaged strategy was to enhance the ability of the state cooperatives to manage or support the economic activities of their members, including productive community enterprises, and to promote new entrepreneurial relationships among them. In this way, a sustainable development organization was to be created within the MNLF community while its members gained in experience and capacity.

Clearly, the resources of the programme were far too small to offer support that would guarantee the participation of the majority of the MNLF members. Targets were established for each state and a limited number of projects were implemented in each of them. Recognizing this, MNLF state leaders felt that it was up to them to do the very best possible with the current projects, in order to guarantee the success of the proposed revolving funds and in hopes of attracting additional funding.

The simplest livelihood projects (e.g. vegetable seed, maize or seaweed production) appeared to be the most successful both in terms of economic impact and confidence building. Some larger projects tended to concentrate resources on a limited number of assets. These projects faced complications as the community organization lacked the skills to effectively manage them, and to guarantee the equitable use and distribution of inputs. Also, a menu-driven approach in implementing assistance programmes without incorporating ideas from beneficiary members and a proper assessment of their needs resulted in some projects not being attuned to the economic potential or needs of the area.

It remained to be seen whether the multipurpose cooperatives structure would prove viable and translate into improved development prospects for its members. This depended on the individual projects that were being implemented, and whether the revolving fund could be efficiently managed. There were also questions about the equity of the support provided under the programme, as the concentration of goods and resources around the MNLF leadership was quite visible.

Further Transition to Development Programming

The Peace Agreement had stipulated a three-year transition period. However, the UN and other assistance programmes for the MNLF did not get to the substantive phase until late 1998. In reality, the transition for the MNLF communities and soldiers was just beginning. There was still debate on the geographical area, the powers that would be granted to the autonomous region, and the viability of the ARMM in view of competing administrative structures and a national policy of decentralization.

The SPCPD was supposed to be an agency designed to manage peace and development efforts within the SZOPAD. However, SPCPD was not given significant resources and, because it was not a constitutional entity, it was not empowered to administer or implement activities. Its role was limited to coordination and it also suffered from the limited capacities of its members.

All of this implied that the UN should be flexible and develop a range of contingencies for the next phase of support. It was thought that the programme should continue since peace was still fragile and MNLF members, after decades of isolation from mainstream society, were just beginning to be integrated into the social, economic and political institutions in Mindanao. Decisions would have to be made as to what extent assistance should continue to target the MNLF and when it should begin to have a broader community focus. It was hoped that the UN system would continue to work in a coordinated programme, and that more donor support would be forthcoming if that was the case.

IV. LESSONS LEARNED

UN activities can contribute greatly to the peace process through the support of confidence building community programmes. Peace-building activities can be a strong niche for the UN system given its comparative advantage as an impartial and recognized institution. However, delays in programme implementation can hinder the peace process and dampen expectations.

- While being active in promoting and implementing its programmes, UNDP should encourage the government to take the lead role in the overall peace-building and development programmes of a region such as Mindanao. The perception of a government not interested or weak can alienate the warring factions who are willing to come to the negotiating table.
- It might be advisable to focus on immediate, short-term projects to engage ex-combatants in employment and income generating activities even when such projects may not be sustainable in the long run. The contribution of such projects to the peace-building efforts can be invaluable.
- In designing and implementing programmes, the needs and requirements of the community should be clearly assessed and taken into consideration. A menu-based approach, while providing for ease in implementation, might not be attuned to community needs and expectations.
- In the face of limited resources, the participation of all key stakeholders in programme design and implementation can help inform the participants of the programme's parameters and limitations, thus bringing down expectations to more realistic levels. Expectation management should be a critical consideration in peace-building exercises.

THE DEVELOPMENT PROGRAMME FOR DISPLACED PERSONS, REFUGEES AND RETURNEES IN CENTRAL AMERICA (PRODERE)

Demobilization and re-integration of soldiers.

PRODERE provides an inspiring example of an innovative and experimental programme in support of a regional peace process which not only served well its direct beneficiaries and their governments, but also became a valuable learning experience for the UN staff members involved and for their respective agencies.

The replication of the PRODERE model in other post-conflict situations is evidence of its success. However, PRODERE was developed and executed in a specific political, social and geographical environment. Therefore, similar initiatives elsewhere have to be adjusted to the historical and political situation of the region or country. Nevertheless, the basic principles on which PRODERE had been designed and implemented were state-of-the-art for any reintegration programme.

I. CONTEXT AND BACKGROUND

As a result of civil conflicts and military activities in El Salvador, Guatemala and Nicaragua during the late 1980s, hundreds of thousands of people lost their lives and more than two million were displaced and forced from their homes. The conflicts affected not only these countries, but the entire Central American region, with intense migratory and refugee flows disturbing the economies, stressing the local social infrastructure capacities and even putting pressure on the social and political structures of the host countries: Belize, Costa Rica, Honduras and Mexico.

In August 1987, the Presidents of Central America met in Guatemala and signed a Peace Plan, known as Esquipulas II, which provided a framework for peace in the region. Governments facing armed conflicts agreed to begin political negotiations with their opposition groups, provide material and legal assistance to the populations affected by the violence, and request international assistance in overcoming their difficult economic situations. In May 1988, the UN General Assembly expressed its support by adopting the Special Plan of Economic Cooperation for Central America (PEC).

Within the framework of the PEC, and with firm backing from Italy, UNDP established the Development Programme for Displaced Persons, Refugees and Returnees in Central America (PRODERE), expanding its existing national project in El Salvador to the regional level. In 1989, at the International Conference on Central American Refugees (CIREFCA), the Government of

Italy confirmed its support for PRODERE by pledging a $115 million grant. With this assistance, PRODERE began its work in 1990 in six Central American countries, in partnership with ILO, UNHCR and WHO/PAHO (Pan American Health Organization). Evaluated by an external team of experts in 1995, PRODERE was praised for its holistic approach to the problem of conflict and displacements and its contribution to the peace process in Central America.

II. PRODERE IN ACTION
The PRODERE Approach and Programme Components
PRODERE initially operated in six countries in the region with the objective of either facilitating the reinsertion of uprooted populations into their communities of origin (El Salvador, Guatemala, Nicaragua) or their long-term integration into their host communities (Belize, Costa Rica, Honduras and Mexico – which was later included in the programme.) The programme was flexible and, over a period of five years, evolved from basically humanitarian assistance to a human development initiative.

PRODERE followed a non-discriminatory, integrated territorial approach in providing assistance to displaced populations. It was designed to promote development as a way of integrating uprooted populations through the rehabilitation of clearly defined geographic areas, which were affected by conflict and/or high levels of displacement. The PRODERE activities were targeted at the communities as a whole without discriminating among refugees, returnees, internally displaced or pre-war populations.

The programme also developed a bottom-up, participatory planning process at the local, municipal and departmental levels which allowed it to respond to the multiple needs of populations affected by conflicts or refugee inflows. It established a network of local Development Committees composed of representatives of the beneficiary population, state ministries and government institutions and local NGOs. Local planning units created within these committees prepared integrated territorial plans for the selected areas. PRODERE emphasized a systematic approach to local health, education, production and job creation projects and encouraged broad-based participation in decision making at every stage.

PRODERE and Reconciliation and Peace Building in Central America
Originating from the Esquipulas Agreement, PRODERE was firmly anchored within the framework of PEC and CIREFCA. This provided PRODERE with an enabling environment in the midst of ongoing turmoil and conflict in the region and allowed it to link its development support with broader concerns for peace and reconciliation. In the PRODERE strategy, the assistance to the uprooted population was seen as inherently dependent on the development of the region, which in turn was clearly linked to the peace and reconciliation process.

The territorial non-discriminatory approach helped PRODERE to maintain its neutrality and a non-partisan profile in complex political situations. This contributed to confidence building at the grassroots level and allowed PRODERE to maintain an open line of communication with government officials, armed opposition groups and local populations in most of the areas of its operation. It helped to forge relationships and collaborations among former enemies, leading to conflict resolution and reconciliation at local and even national levels. For example, in Nicaragua, the Sandinista Army handed the military base, Estanacia Cora, over to UNDP in a meeting at which the National Resistance was present. The base then became a training centre.

The PRODERE-initiated participatory planning process and community level discussions on development priorities also enabled people in ex-conflict areas to come together and build new partnerships on the basis of shared concerns and objectives. The local development committees and planning units, by virtue of their broad-based participation, provided humanitarian spaces for conflict resolution and peace making. In many communities dialogue and consensus building emerged for the first time. These mechanisms created a sense of inclusion among populations historically excluded from the political process, addressing the underlying causes of conflict and social and political unrest in these countries. However, while PRODERE put emphasis on the situation of children and the status of indigenous populations, it did not pay equal attention to the needs of women and in particular to their participation in the decision-making and peace processes.

PRODERE initiatives strengthened civil society at the grassroots level by increasing people's participation in municipal and local development committees. The participation of civil society in the decision-making process at all levels particularly helped reduce public fear of contacts with the state and government authorities, and helped to redefine and strengthen the relationship between civil society and the governments. For example, in El Salvador, PRODERE activities led to joint work between the Ministry of Education and the Farabundo Marti National Liberation (FMLN). In Guatemala, the programme's support for the accreditation of popular teachers trained in the refugee camps led to their incorporation in the public education system.

In a complex regional context, PRODERE's impact on peace building and reconciliation processes varied among countries, and at different points in time in the same country. Despite the fact that the conflict in Nicaragua ended in 1989, two years before the end of the El Salvadoran war, and when peace was yet to be achieved in Guatemala, PRODERE's contribution to peace was most controversial in Nicaragua. When participatory decision-making processes were introduced for the first time in the highly politicized context of post-conflict Nicaragua, PRODERE was not able to immediately establish a non-partisan profile and its contribution to the country's peace process suffered as a result. However, PRODERE learned from its experience and later successfully brought the Contras, Sandinista government and NGO representatives together through its local and municipal level development committees in its areas of operation.

A noteworthy contribution of PRODERE to the peace and reconciliation process in the region was its critical role in the creation of Guatemala's National Peace Fund (FONAPAZ), which paved the way for peace talks between the Government of Guatemala and the armed opposition groups. FONAPAZ adopted the basic PRODERE methodology of participatory bottom-up planning and human development at the local level. In Guatemala, land occupancy was a critical issue, since areas of conflict were being occupied by returnees and other settlers who were not necessarily the original residents. Much of the land once worked by Guatemalan refugees in Mexico was in the hands of IDPs, who left their home areas during the years of violence. Both PRODERE and FONAPAZ, through their focus on participatory bottom-up planning processes, addressed critical land issues at the community level.

PRODERE and the Promotion of Human Rights in Central America

One of the main features of PRODERE was the inclusion of concern for human rights as one of the programme components. Considered initially as a documentation and legalization programme, the component became a broad-based human rights initiative, successfully expanding the debate on human rights from political concerns to economic, social and cultural dimensions and thus shifting the focus from displacement to one of general human development.

In fact, PRODERE activities played a key role in changing people's attitudes towards human rights and made discussions and debates on human rights issues more acceptable. Furthermore, discourse was shifted as human rights was introduced as a development issue to both local governments and communities. Historically, the theme of human rights had a subversive connotation, particularly where the armed forces' repressive actions were guided by the national security doctrine. The broad-based participation and discussions initiated under PRODERE questioned the institutional monopoly of the warring forces in many areas and contributed to making human rights an important concern and a basic need felt by the entire community.

PRODERE provided support to national human rights institutions for the decentralization and promotion of basic human rights at local levels and organized training programmes and technical assistance for the human rights monitors. Local human rights systems were also created throughout the areas of programme intervention. However, there was doubt regarding the sustainability of many of PRODERE's human rights initiatives. The institutional and financial weaknesses of many of the organizations supported under the programme was a major concern and the effectiveness of the training provided was questioned.

PRODERE and the Needs of the Uprooted Populations in Central America

The PRODERE approach of non-discrimination helped the uprooted populations undergo reinsertion and integration into their communities in a more peaceful manner. The focus on community-based development activities and the integrated territorial approach also generated economic, social and political conditions conducive to a peaceful and sustainable reinsertion of displaced persons into normal life. The return-to-work approach, linking reinsertion with economic activities, created a culture of work, replacing a culture of violence and unrest. PRODERE's territorial approach also reduced the dominance of military strategy by repositioning investment decisions in production, social and physical infrastructures to respond to needs and economic efficiency rather than counter-insurgency criteria.

However, the most noteworthy contribution of PRODERE in this area had been its impact on national policies relating to uprooted populations and issues of displacement. In El Salvador, Guatemala and Nicaragua, during periods of intense conflict the problem of displacement was considered as a national security problem. The needs of uprooted populations, often considered as a military threat, were addressed within a counter-insurgency framework rather than as a humanitarian problem. Military authorities controlled access to and resettlement of civilian communities. By supporting the demands of the uprooted populations to return home to demilitarized communities, PRODERE helped to change the official population settlement policies. PRODERE also advocated a policy of voluntary return of all uprooted populations, formation of civil patrols and the absence of military accompaniment. Although it faced military opposition in the beginning, PRODERE was ultimately able to effect all these changes in the entire region, shifting the balance of command away from military towards civilian authorities.

In El Salvador and Nicaragua, these policy changes accelerated as conflicts came to an end. In Guatemala, PRODERE concentrated on giving broad support to the safe return of uprooted populations to their communities. It was critical in guaranteeing the rights of the Communities of Popular Resistance (CPR), a remote indigenous community in Guatemala considered by the military authority as a guerrilla force, to be documented and considered as a civilian population, and facilitated the return of its members to their communities.

PRODERE's interventions with displaced persons in Central America made it a major actor in this field in the region and contributed to a change in policy. The treatment of the uprooted populations by national governments was no longer left to the sole discretion of these governments. Thanks to PRODERE and its substantial donor support, the countries' handling of the uprooted populations became a benchmark by which the international community monitored progress towards democratization and human development.

PRODERE, UN Coordination and Institutional Learning

Executed by UNDP/OPS, PRODERE was the first regional project to have four agencies of the UN system (ILO, UNDP, UNHCR, WHO/PAHO) participate in one programme. Prior to PRODERE, inter-agency collaboration in this area was weak and focused only on short-term projects. PRODERE's experience was a learning process for each of the participating agencies and for the UN system in general. Mutual respect by agencies for each other's area of competence became a working principle.

The partnership developed between UNHCR and UNDP under PRODERE is particularly noteworthy.The PRODERE experience contributed to the formation of a joint UNDP/UNHCR working group, which played a significant role in defining key issues and policy recommendations. Of course inter-agency collaboration varied depending on the phases of the programme. During the initial phases, UNDP and UNHCR cooperation was crucial and at the later stage, ILO and UNDP worked together on local development initiatives.

The Question of Replicability

In addition to the large-scale CARERE programme in Cambodia, PRODERE-like initiatives have been undertaken in many countries, mostly in Africa. However, it is worth noting that the success of PRODERE to a large extent was due to the political environment of the Central American region at the time it was instituted, as defined by the Esquipulas Agreement and the subsequent PEC and CIREFCA initiatives.

PRODERE and the Relief-Development Continuum

PRODERE evolved over its five-year period from a humanitarian assistance programme to a major development undertaking. The progress from relief to development could be analysed in terms of different phases that the programme went through from its inception in late 1989 to its completion in 1995. During the first phase (1989-1991) of its operation, PRODERE concentrated on developing national programmes and providing humanitarian assistance to communities in identified priority areas. The goal at this stage was to build credibility and the space necessary to operate in conflict and refugee zones by focusing on immediate impact activities for resettlement and integration of uprooted populations. During this phase, a top-down approach was followed with very little community participation in identifying problems and programme priorities. PRODERE was, however, able to move away from this supply side approach and evolve into a demand sensitive programme during its next phase in 1991. This was due to a UNDP/OPS decision to decentralize operations to the field offices in intervention areas. With decentralization, PRODERE was able to relate to ongoing parallel initiatives such as various health and human rights programmes, and hence broaden its scope of activities.

The evolution of PRODERE was also facilitated by the development of local level participatory planning mechanisms and integrated development strategies. By recognizing the importance of local participation and consensus in decision making, PRODERE was able to establish itself as a human development programme at the local level.

III. LESSONS LEARNED

- PRODERE, a pilot initiative, achieved success at the local level. However, stronger linkages between local and national bodies is required to transform local successes into national programmes benefiting the entire population. National recognition and ownership of programmes is also important in ensuring sustainability.

- PRODERE success in promoting human development at local levels led to similar UNDP interventions in other regions, including in some of the countries covered in this report. However, it needs to be highlighted that approaches and structures cannot be transferred by simply copying a programme from elsewhere without careful adaptation to the given situation. Programme success is context-specific and geography-specific.

- PRODERE's success owes much to the high level of collaboration among the UN agencies. The strong commitment and smooth coordination exhibited by the UN agencies should be further examined and promoted in developing PRODERE-like programmes in other post-conflict regions of the world.

- Participatory, community-based, bottom-up programme approaches do not only help respond to the multiple needs of populations affected by conflicts and encourage local commitment to programme success. By bringing together disparate groups of people to share ideas and concerns, they also create a sense of inclusion, address the root causes of conflict and hence make possible long-lasting peace.

- When formulating post-conflict reintegration programmes, gender issues should be incorporated as an important programme component since women normally comprise a large percentage of the uprooted populations.

- In the process of establishing peace, human rights issues should be given important consideration. The concept of human rights, in such cases, should go beyond the confines of violation of political rights alone to include demands for basic social, economic and cultural rights of the uprooted populations.

- PRODERE's evolution from a humanitarian programme to a development initiative is particularly noteworthy. With its emphasis on community participation, it provided a foundation for a human development process in areas where unsustainable territorial development plans had been applied, often in response to the exigencies of the "national security doctrine." In the context of relief-development continuum, the PRODERE experience shows that it is critical and feasible to go beyond the resumption of traditional development activities, and to reassess and provide the basis for a people-centred development process.

REPORT ON SOMALIA

David Cough/UNDP

Port of Berbera, undergoing rehabilitation.

In Somalia, a country characterized by the absence of any central government for over a decade, the international community faced great difficulties in efforts to sustain peace, deliver humanitarian relief and support reintegration and re-establishment of basic structures of local government.

UNDP has been involved in aid coordination and has supported programmes of rehabilitation and development, responding to the opportunities of the situation rather than following pre-conceived development plans. On the whole, this was seen as a useful contribution to the promotion of peace building and to the wellbeing of the people of Somalia.

Country Update

After more than ten years of disorder and violence, Somalia has not rid itself of such affliction, with continuous dire economic problems, unmet humanitarian needs, unstable politics and an unpredictable security situation. The Somali Peace Conference (known as the Arta process) led to the election of a Transitional Parliament and President in August 2000, followed by the formation of a Transitional National Government (TNG). The TNG, however, has not been able so far to extend the peace process and adequately bring in other players, nor has it succeeded in extending its authority beyond limited parts of Mogadishu. In order to push the peace process forward a January 2002 International Authority on Development (IGAD) resolution called for the holding of a National Reconciliation Conference for Somalia during the second half of 2002.

In 2001, some $100 million of humanitarian and development aid was disbursed to Somalia, half through the UN system. As the UN agencies operating in Somalia are based across the border in Kenya, the provision of assistance is all the more complex and costly. In such an operation, the role played by the Somalia Aid Coordination Body (SACB), which has been revitalized and now counts more than 120 member organizations, continues to be critical and exemplary. The SACB is supported by the UN System at all levels. The RC/HC is the Chair of its Steering Committee and Deputy Chair of its Executive Committee where policy frameworks and security matters are coordinated. Moreover the SACB secretariat is ensured by the UN Coordination Unit (UNCU), which is also playing a key role in supporting the RC/HC and in providing information, analysis and policy support to the UN system and development partners.

Under the leadership of the RC/HC, internal UN coordination mechanisms have also been strengthened and recently expanded and now include, beyond the regular UN Heads of Agencies coordination meetings and the more operational UN Joint Working Group (JWG), two new coordination and information sharing mechanisms established in 2001, namely: (i) a Weekly Analysis Group – a forum used by the RC/HC, UNPOS and the UN Security Team to analyse the political, operational and security impact of weekly development in Somalia; and (ii) a UN Human Rights and Gender Joint Working Group.

UNDP's activities in Somalia are multi-sectoral with a long term outlook striving to bridge the gap between relief and development and to foster an enabling environment for Sustainable Human Development (SHD). UNDP has three priority areas in Somalia: peace and security; governance; and economic recovery/poverty reduction. In order to reduce extreme poverty, an Economic Recovery and Poverty Reduction programme is now being launched that will promote economic growth and encourage the economic empowerment of vulnerable populations. This programme is linked to the "Watching Brief" being established by UNDP jointly with the World Bank and the IMF.

Source: UNDP Regional Bureau for Arab States

I. CONTEXT AND BACKGROUND

As a country without a national government, Somalia presented special challenges to UNDP. After the fall of President Siad Barre in January 1991, the country descended into chaos. Vying for power, the many militia groups that emerged to fill the vacuum divided the country along kinship lines, with rule based on clan and regional enclaves. An international military intervention undertaken from 1992 to 1995 by the United Nations Operations in Somalia (UNOSOM) and the United Nations Task Force (UNITAF) failed to secure peace. When UNOSOM and UNITAF left in 1995, the political, social and economic situation in Somalia was little better than when the international community had entered the fray.

The nature of displacement in Somalia was highly complicated. Predominantly nomadic, Somalis left their settlements almost readily. An overwhelming majority of the population migrated or was forced to flee at some time, driven by lack of food, conflict, drought and easier access to aid. The U. S. Agency for International Development (USAID) estimated the number of IDPs in 1996 at 250,000 and rising, while the UN counted over 1,000,000 IDPs in 1997. After more than a decade of war, there were an estimated 350,000 Somali refugees in Djibouti, Ethiopia, Kenya, Libya and Yemen.

Since 1995, the country has witnessed three distinct regional trends: recovery, crisis and transition, mainly conforming to geography. The south is still in crisis. The north is experiencing varying degrees of recovery, most notably in the northwest, or Somaliland, which has *de facto* seceded under President Egal but lacks international recognition, while some other regions are in tentative transition. Northeast Somalia proclaimed itself the autonomous state of Puntland and has clan-based conflicts over the demarcated border with Somaliland. Mogadishu-based faction leaders divided the capital into respective spheres of influence and the security situation there remains in a fragile state. Regional peace keeping efforts backed by the Organization of African Unity (OAU), the Intergovernmental Authority on Development (IGAD) and individual countries did endeavour to bring the various factions together, but had limited success.

II. RESPONSES
UN in Somalia

The work of the UN in Somalia in the early 1990s came under criticism from many quarters. The international military intervention under UNOSOM and UNITAF was considered a failed operation. The UN effort was beset with internal difficulties, fuelled by political issues, and a general lack of preparation.

Despite the setback, the UN agencies continued to work in Somalia. Most, but not all, of the agencies, donors and NGOs ran their Somali programmes from Nairobi, Kenya with project level activities and sub-offices in secure areas within Somalia. This presented coordination problems. UNDP, at the time of this study, was developing a regional programme to support reintegration, to be implemented by IGAD, based in Addis Ababa. The UN Political Office on Somalia (UNPOS) was based in Nairobi. Representing the UN Secretary-General, UNPOS's role was to monitor and facilitate a political resolution of the Somali conflict. The UNDP RR/RC, also in Nairobi, served as humanitarian coordinator (UNHC), representing the UN Office for the Coordination of Humanitarian Affairs (OCHA).

The United Nations Country Team (UNCT) was strengthened in 1998 by a special UNDP grant in an effort to enhance UN-coordinated action, apart from that carried out by the Somalia Aid Coordination Body (SACB). SACB was made up of various bilateral and multilateral aid agencies, UN operational agencies and NGOs. In addition, the RC set up a system of UN focal points within the country, an initiative required for country level coordination and planning.

UNDP Response

Somalia has been an extremely complex case and a challenge for conflict and post-conflict programming. With no government as its counterpart, UNDP had to identify Somali partners in an extremely volatile and unstable situation and all projects had to be implemented by UN implementing agencies. In northwest Somaliland (a zone of recovery), UNDP worked with local authorities, though there were legal obstacles to having the traditional UNDP relationship with government. In the northeast and some areas in the south (Zones of Transition), relations with local counterparts developed as political stability allowed for the beginning of economic recovery, though the fragility of the situation and intra- and inter-clan rivalries frequently set back initiatives. The Zones of Crisis such as central and southern Somalia, including Mogadishu were characterized by recurrent emergencies and the lack of legitimate political authorities, and required the delivery of basic humanitarian assistance under high-risk situations.

UNDP Programmes

The UNDP programmes in Somalia were developed in response to the country's very special and unique circumstances. To be effective, UNDP needed to have the capacity to respond to immediate opportunities, while trying to place its interventions within a developmental framework. In the absence of a government, UNDP worked with three sectors of Somali society: civil, economic and emerging public institutions. Almost all UNDP programming in Somalia could be seen as responding to the needs of war-affected populations, directly or indirectly. As the zones of recovery expanded, there was increasing interest in support for local administrative structures and processes to strengthen the emerging decentralized mode of governance. Obviously, this approach faced questions as to the viability of a shift from reintegration and rehabilitation to support for planning processes and governance while basic needs were still far from being met. On the other hand, there was hardly any prospect for starting self-reliant development without participatory community organization.

Reintegration

The Somalia Rehabilitation Programme (SRP) was initiated in 1993 as an area-based project (initially called Somalia Rural Rehabilitation Programme {SRRP}) to promote peace and reconciliation through support for the economic and social recovery of war- affected communities. The SRP accounted for about one third of UNDP resources for Somalia ($30 million) since 1993. The programme started in the northwest (Somaliland) and the northeast in 1993. In 1994 it was expanded to the southwest, with a project office across the Somali border in Kenya, and in 1997 a programme was started in central Somalia. Over 500 sub-projects were supported, including rehabilitation of social infrastructure; training of health and education workers; improving access to water for drinking, livestock and irrigation; road construction; rehabilitation of public buildings; distribution of agricultural inputs and tools; and support for small rural enterprises. However, it was difficult for the SRP to maintain coherence as an integrated project, given the diverse conditions across the country.

The Somali Civil Protection Project comprised three elements: de-mining, law enforcement/police training and reintegration of ex-combatants. At the time of the study, the only component that had been initiated was mine clearance in Somaliland. This project was highly praised by the Somaliland government and key donors. It was unusual to place all three components within the same programme. If a demobilization programme were to be developed in Somaliland by UNDP it should probably have been administratively separated from the mine clearance project.

UNDOS (UN Development Office for Somalia) was a key UNDP project that provided a policy and planning base for UN agencies and other donors to use in developing their Somali programmes. The Local Administrative Structures Unit focused on good governance, undertaking needs assessments and providing technical assistance and training. The Development Planning Unit collected and analysed socio-economic data, while the Information Unit had Geographic Information System (GIS) capacity that served UN agencies, NGOs and bilateral agencies by mapping data on health, water supply, crop patterns, flood conditions, etc. UNDOS also served as the secretariat for SACB.

Rehabilitation of Seaports and Airport. Maritime activity is key to Somali economic survival and recovery. With more than 3,000 km. of coastline, there are major ports – Mogadishu, Kismayo, Berbera and Bosasso – and a number of smaller seasonal ports. The ports continue to generate revenue for local governments and are the main outlet for import and export trade not only for Somalia but also for Ethiopia. Through UNCTAD and USAID, UNDP supported the rehabilitation of the ports in Berbera and Bosasso. The project was important in developing port management capacities and the introduction of internationally accepted standards.

In the absence of a Somali national government, the UN Secretariat, the International Civil Aviation Organization (ICAO) and UNDP worked together to provide support safety for international air transport operations into and through Somali airspace. The Civil Aviation Caretaker Authority for Somalia (CACAS), operated from Nairobi, and had assisted in the rehabilitation of airports in Belet Weyne, Berbera, Borama, Bossaso, Hargeisa and Kalabayd.

III. LESSONS LEARNED

- UNDP and the Department of Political Affairs (DPA) must have a close working relationship and consultative practice in countries in political crisis, such as Somalia, safeguarding cooperation while respecting each other's respective mandates.
- When a coordination body already exists, like SACB, it is in the spirit of UN reform to work with and strengthen that broader body rather than to invest in developing a parallel coordinating body.
- Mine clearance, police training and demobilization of ex-combatants, though all related to public safety, require different specific skills and institutional counterparts. It is better to separate them out rather than to place them within an umbrella project.
- Area-based programmes, such as SRP, should put the highest emphasis on specific assessment of needs in the areas of operations when developing their strategies and work plans.
- Special attention to UNDP performance in conflict-prone countries and close headquarters backstopping for country offices are required. If tensions arise within the UNDP field staff or in relation to government authorities and the international community, UNDP should be ready to examine the situation and take remedial action.

REPORT ON TAJIKISTAN

Voluntary repatriation of women who fled the conflict

After gaining independence in 1992, Tajikistan got mired in internal conflict, with fragile peace efforts supported by the United Nations. The 1997 peace agreement gave hope and direction to these efforts. Its success, however, was much dependent on assistance from the international community.

UNDP made a valuable contribution, both in capacity building at the central level and with downstream projects of peace building and rehabilitation at the community level. This combined approach was considered useful for promoting the peace process and for rehabilitation and reconstruction of the country.

I. CONTEXT AND BACKGROUND

In 1992, shortly after gaining independence in the wake of the dissolution of the former USSR, Tajikistan descended into a bloody civil war as different regional and political groups struggled to fill a power vacuum. By mid 1993, in a country of less than six million people, an estimated 60,000 had been killed, some 600,000 had been displaced internally and over 60,000 had crossed the border into Afghanistan. Many others fled to neighbouring Central Asian republics, as well as to other countries in the CIS. The armed conflict with the resultant massive displacement of farm communities also put a heavy toll on the productive base and social structure of Tajikistan's already weakened economy,

Country Update

In Tajikistan, UNDP places a high priority on poverty reduction. Recent poor harvests, severe drought, and the inadequate funding of basic social services have increased the already high levels of poverty and human suffering, particularly in the rural areas. In monetary terms, real wages have fallen dramatically to less than five per cent of pre-independence levels, with state employees receiving only an average of US$9 equivalent per month. Based on the needs and priorities of Tajikistan, activities of the country office are being closely integrated within a broad framework of support to the country's poverty reduction strategy.

Special attention has been given to efforts to establish linkages between poverty reduction and governance issues during the implementation of the new Phase II of the Tajikistan Rehabilitation, Reconstruction and Development Programme (RRDP). In addition to the infrastructure investments, which were a major part of RRDP support during Phase I, from 1996 to 2001, increased priority is being given to strengthening of local governance structures and practices, and Small and Medium Enterprise (SME) development. UNDP is managing an area-based development approach aimed at rehabilitating infrastructure and services; reintegrating ex-combatants and returnees; and helping communities address new cross-border issues (especially water supply). The programme relies on subcontracting local public and private firms in order to stimulate local economies and create jobs. In addition, UNDP has introduced self-financing and decentralized management approaches to ensure that rehabilitated schools, health centres, hospitals, and water and irrigation systems operate on a sustainable basis. UNDP also provides support to bringing environmental issues into the national development agenda.   Source: UNDP Tajikistan Country Office struggling with transition to a market economy.

A complex process of peace negotiations between the Government of Tajikistan (GoT) and the United Tajik Opposition (UTO) was initiated under the auspices of the UN in early 1994. The talks reached a successful conclusion in June 1997, with the signing of the General Agreement on Peace and Reconciliation by both GoT and UTO. The General Agreement provided the framework for the political, social and economic reconstruction of the country after five years of civil war. Immediately after the signing of the General Agreement, the Commission on National Reconciliation (CNR) was established to implement the Agreement over a transitional period of 12 to 18 months.

However, after early 1998, sporadic but repeated incidents of hostilities, political instability and in particular, the killing of a number of international aid workers, including United Nations Mission of Observers (UNMOT) personnel, jeopardized the peace process and shook the faith of the international community in its successful completion.

II. RESPONSES

The United Nations system was involved early on in establishing peace through facilitating reconciliation among the fighting parties. The 1997 General Agreement on Peace and Reconciliation ushered in the prospect of rebuilding the country with renewed commitment from all. However, the task remained an uphill struggle. During the long years of conflict, the government lost effective control. The absence of security threatened all, seriously affecting development work. Donor interest also flagged due to the slow take-off of development momentum.

The donor community had largely been withholding its material assistance, claiming the lack of security, which was indeed one of the symptoms of the crisis situation. Under these circumstances, it was encouraging to observe the dedication and determination of the representatives of the international community present within the country, who carried on with their onerous mandate of peace building. In a rare unity of purpose and synchronized efforts, the United Nations system undertook an impressive array of projects in spite of the very limited resources available.

The Programmes

Refugees. UNHCR repatriated some 43,000 refugees from Afghanistan. The failure of the peace negotiations to reach any conclusive agreement by 1994 resulted in UNHCR's downsizing its repatriation programme in 1995. The programmes of rehabilitation, implemented through Quick Impact Projects (QIPs), were handed over to the Organization for Security and Cooperation in Europe (OSCE) and UNDP. Throughout 1995-1997, a period of uncertainty prevailed due largely to the deterioration of security conditions.

From the end of 1997, the situation improved significantly. UNHCR was able to repatriate the remaining 20,000 refugees from Afghanistan (Mazar-i-Sharif and Kunduz areas) and renewed its part in the rehabilitation programme. UNDP addressed the problems of sustainable reintegration through the Community Development Centres (CDCs) and the Rehabilitation, Reconstruction and Development Programme (RRDP).

IDPs. The exact number of IDPs still awaiting rehabilitation was not known. The existence of economic and urban migrants added to the confusion. The problems facing IDPs were largely considered as less urgent than those of the other two targeted groups, refugees and demobilized combatants. Some IDP returnees benefited from the then existing programmes of reintegration.

Demobilized combatants. The key to stability was demobilization and the implementation of effective programmes for the reintegration of the demobilized forces. Unfortunately, demobilization had not yet taken place on a large scale despite being addressed in the peace process. The military protocol of the General Agreement envisaged threefold activities: repatriation, assembly and disarmament; storage of arms; and integration. Nevertheless, the process was flawed due to delays and uncertainty about the terms of a general amnesty. Other factors contributing to the rather unsuccessful demobilization programme were as follows: the power sharing agreement had not yet been fully implemented and there was no power sharing at the local level; there were divisive tendencies within the opposition; and the number of fighters had been exaggerated as the demobilization process became a political bargaining tool.

There was a feeling that development programmes should have been immediately taken up in the assembly areas of the fighters. The agencies under UNDP leadership were prepared to assist, as far as their resources would allow. As there was little chance for land distribution, the two options were the RRDP type of public works rehabilitation programmes, and the ILO-proposed initiative to create small-scale enterprises. In any case, incentives had to be provided to the ex-combatants to engage in these rehabilitation options. Another issue that had not been yet solved was the proposed weapons buy-back programme, an idea that was welcomed by all but which lacked financial support.

III. UNDP ACTIVITIES

Between June and August 1997, UNDP reviewed its strategy and worked on three principal areas: aid co-ordination, peace building and the RRDP. The strengthening of local communities for project implementation, expansion of the Women in Development programme (WID) and peace building through CDCs were given particular attention. To enhance UNDP's capacity for work in the field, sub-offices were created in Gharm, Kulyab, Shartuz and the Zarafshan valley through a decentralization strategy that began in late 1996.

Rehabilitation, Reconstruction and Development Programme (RRDP). Since 1996, UNDP had been supporting rehabilitation and reconstruction activities in war-affected regions under its RRDP. This was a multi-sectoral community-based initiative, concentrating its efforts on restoration of basic infrastructure and stimulation of economic activities in war-torn rural communities. Under the RRDP, programme implementation offices were set up in the target areas and annual work plans were formulated to generate social and economic activities.

RRDP functioned as a cost-efficient public works department, rebuilding and rehabilitating schools, hospitals and health posts, drinking water systems, etc. in close cooperation with district development committees, involving the local authorities and representatives of returnees and women. Contracts were awarded to local contractors on the basis of tender. At the same time, the government authorities made a small piece of land available to school and hospital employees (0.2 ha. per staff member) to ensure maintenance and create income for schoolteachers, doctors and other professional staff.

The Peace-building Programme. Efforts had been made to build confidence and create an enabling environment for peace and reconciliation at the community level. The programme operated in areas with large numbers of IDPs, refugees and ex-combatants from different ethnic and religious backgrounds. It developed a participatory process of bringing together people of varied backgrounds by working on community development issues and activities of mutual interest. Based on the idea of promoting a culture of peace and understanding, it created a number of local NGOs in the spirit of initiating community service activities channelled to the grassroots level. The first of these were youth clubs with cultural activities and sports. Later, Community Development Centres offered a wide range of social and economic programmes.

UNHCR Handover. UNDP's management of the move from UNHCR's QIP repatriation assistance to activities with the desired development momentum was achieved with mixed results. Some external factors other than security (e.g. vested interests in certain economic fields and lack of funding) resulted in the failure of some programmes. However, in Kofarnihon, a women's programme did very well, with Women in Development (WID) bureau cells created in all locations.

UNDP Leadership. The 1997 recovery, initiated with experienced professional leadership from within UNDP, was remarkable. Added to this was a new understanding within the UN team of the reality of having to coexist in a very trying situation. The RR emerged as the key authority, combining in one person the roles of the RC, HC, Deputy SRSG and facilitator of support to the Council for National Reconciliation.

IV. LESSONS LEARNED

- Under conditions of deteriorating security, donors are reluctant to commit resources for peace building when they are needed the most. It is in such situations that the UN System needs to take a leadership role in working in the country and with the donors to reopen and direct peace negotiations.

- In conflict situations involving a large number of combatants, demobilization is key to ushering in stability. Programmes should be directed to the immediate reintegration of the demobilized. Reconstruction projects such as the rebuilding of schools, roads, hospitals and drinking water systems can help engage ex-combatants and spur economic activity in war affected regions.

- In the peace-building effort, the participation of local NGOs and community members, especially youth should be included, given their familiarity with local conditions and their ability to work at the grassroots level to engender trust and cooperation.

- In taking over UNHCR's Quick Impact Projects, UNDP should be selective, mindful of its Sustainable Human Development mandate and financial resources.

III. SUMMARY OF LESSONS LEARNED

UNDP, through its involvement in crises and post-conflict situations in various regions and countries throughout the world, has accumulated much experience in coordinating and implementing reintegration, rehabilitation and reconstruction activities. While no two situations can be the same, the experiences as presented in the country reports, provide a wealth of knowledge with valuable insights toward better future planning and management of activities in the aftermath of violent conflicts. Two key overriding lessons appear from the reports. First, humanitarian assistance and development cooperation do not follow a consecutive linear progression but rather should be viewed in the totality of a given situation. Peace, reintegration and development should all be considered as critical components and objectives of post-conflict management, co-existing synergistically. Second, conflicts are inherently contextual, shaped by the political, economic, geographic and socio-cultural conditions of the region or country. While the lessons learned and experiences gained elsewhere can certainly be utilized, post-conflict policies and programmes should not be imported wholesale from another "similar" situation but rather, carefully designed and implemented, understanding the specific context and needs of the direct beneficiary population. This requires local participation, ownership and capacity building to ensure programme and project relevance and sustainability.

Certain underlying observations and lessons learned run through the reports, providing common ground in understanding and planning for post-conflict situations.

REINTEGRATION AND RECONSTRUCTION ACTIVITIES

■ Economic growth and employment generation hold the key to a successful and effective process of reintegration. Where ex-combatants, refugees and IDPs form a large portion of the population, it is better to target activities on the entire community as it makes programme implementation easier and avoids opposition and alienation from community members who otherwise would not be targeted.

■ Targeting reintegration activities, whether on specific groups or on specific communities, can only be a limited strategy for reintegration. This approach has to be complemented by more general efforts to stimulate long-term growth and employment in the entire region or country.

■ In the immediate aftermath of a conflict, it might be advisable to focus on short-term Quick Impact Projects (QIPs) to engage demobilized soldiers, refugees and IDPs in employment and income generating activities even when such projects may not be sustainable in the long run. The contribution of such projects to the peace-building and reconciliation efforts can be invaluable. Reconstruction of basic infrastructure such as roads, hospitals, schools and water supply systems can employ large numbers of people and provide immediate benefit to the population.

■ However, at the same time, special attention should be given to developing long-term programmes that directly address the underlying causes of instability. Often, regions of conflict lack skilled human resources and the financial wherewithal critical to programme sustainability. Training of locals, accessible credit schemes and national ownership can go a long way in building local and national capacities to sustain a growing number of programmes.

■ Time is of the essence is delivering humanitarian and development programmes to those affected by conflicts. Governments, donors and implementing agencies have to act quickly to prevent further escalation of war and to provide relief to the victims. Delays can not only exacerbate the situation on site but lead to negative perceptions of international assistance.

■ Continual and thorough assessment of needs at the local, regional and national levels, and on-going programme evaluation and monitoring are equally important in achieving programme success.

■ Programmes and projects should leave room for contingencies. Crises and post-conflict situations are not always predictable and programmes need to be vigilant and adaptive to the changing environment. Otherwise they might be rendered irrelevant or lack support from other organizations and local communities. Abrupt changes in the environment can lead to implementation delays and major changes in programme costs.

UNDP'S ROLE AND PERFORMANCE

■ UNDP, given its in-country presence, outstanding global reputation as an impartial, objective development partner and mandate for sustainable human development has a strong comparative advantage in playing a leadership role in managing post-conflict situations. The UNDP resident representative, who is also normally the resident coordinator, is in a privileged position to take the leading role in coordinating international assistance.

■ Coordination among humanitarian and development partners is critical in managing crises and post-conflict situations. UNDP needs to work with UN agencies, multilaterals such as the World Bank and bilateral donors in a cooperative spirit in building strategies and implementing programmes. Joint programming arrangements have to be clearly formulated and a trust fund established under UNDP to achieve further collaboration, accountability and operational ease.

- Inter-agency working committees need to clearly delineate roles for each agency to avoid "turf" wars, minimize resource wastage and ensure timely implementation. Similarly, UNDP needs to work with local and international NGOs as they often have strong formal and informal linkages at the grass-roots level and hence can better implement programmes and projects.

- UNDP needs to be flexible in its operating modalities. National execution might not always be possible, especially in countries where the government is weak or absent and when programmes have to be implemented immediately. As in Bosnia and Herzegovina, UNDP might have to work with local and municipal bodies if there are too many international agencies working at the national level.

- For effective UNDP involvement, country offices need to be adequately funded and staffed with competent personnel who have the required knowledge of local conditions and experience in crises and post-conflict management. Heavy dependence on headquarters can unnecessarily delay implementation, especially when headquarters has a lack of appreciation for the imperatives of post-conflict assistance and maintains a "business-as-usual" approach during the early phase of UNDP intervention.

- UNDP's strength in national capacity-building activities such as managing general elections, setting up national and local government institutions, forming security structures by establishing trained police forces and coordinating de-mining activities needs to be highlighted and further emphasized.

A "GOOD PRACTICE" SCENARIO

On the basis of the lessons learned from the country studies, a "good practice" scenario can be set forth as follows. As a generic guideline, this has been idealized and simplified for the sake of illustration:

- Post-conflict needs are identified through an internationally mandated, multi-organizational assessment team. The needs and possible assistance are discussed and confirmed by government officials in accordance with the relevant objectives, policies and procedures. The UNDP country office is associated with these discussions as appropriate. Donors confirm their intentions to contribute for specific programmes and projects.

- In assessing needs and designing programmes to meet those needs, beneficiary participation is highly encouraged. Attention is given to local vs. regional or national needs, targeting of certain groups vs. community based programmes and to issues of gender and ethnicity.

- Pre-feasibility studies and relevant information and data are brought together. Beneficiaries and local experts recruited for the purpose are associated closely with the technical studies, along with UNDP and other international and donor organizations present. If at this stage it is thought that UNOPS or another entity is likely to execute the programme, the executing partner is also associated with the study and ensuing policy formulation.

■ Specific attention is given to the technical and management capacities needed to maintain and operate the infrastructure once it has been rehabilitated, including the question of institution building (public utilities, for example), cost recovery schemes and possible governance issues. Appropriate parallel projects addressing these matters and complementing the physical rehabilitation project are prepared and submitted for funding to the donors. For greater impact, and added value, logical linkages are made with other programmes in the same geographical areas.

■ Following the decision and agreement to fund the programme through UNDP, and formulation of programme document(s), approval is obtained on a pre-established "fast track" sequence, with pre-established time frames for each step and each party involved. Progress is closely monitored by UNDP for programmes under its sponsorship. It ensures that all parties to the programme are fully briefed on their roles, responsibilities and commitments, as well as those of the other partners, and that these are all clearly and fully spelled out and agreed to in relevant signed agreements and programme documents. UNDP's responsibilities in particular are fully explained, notably as they relate to other parties in the agreement(s).

As conflicts erupt and subside in various corners of the world, the international community is under pressure to be actively involved in peace building, reintegration and reconstruction efforts. Countries in conflict are usually poor and in dire need of immediate financial, technical and material aid. However, limiting international engagement to humanitarian operations does not address the underlying inequalities and inequities that give rise to conflict situations, and can sometimes have the unintended consequence of prolonging the war itself. Increasingly it is being realized that development is not only necessary for people to achieve better living standards and increased life choices but that it is essential to preventing conflicts and preserving peace. Ensuring that development reaches every community and individual is our greatest challenge today.

ABBREVIATIONS AND ACRONYMS

ADB	African Development Bank /Asian Development Bank
ADRA	Adventist Development and Relief Agency (Japan)
ADS	area development scheme
ALD	activities of limited duration
ARS	area rehabilitation scheme
CAP	Consolidated Interagency Appeal
CARERE	Cambodia Resettlement and Reintegration Programme
CCA	Common Country Assessment
CCF	Country Cooperation Framework
CDC	community development centre
CIS	Commonwealth of Independent States
CPC	Country in Crisis and/or Post-Conflict Situation
CTA	Chief Technical Advisor
DAC	Development Assistance Committee
DDSMS	Department for Development Support and Management Services
DESA	Department of Economic and Social Affairs
DEX	direct execution
DHA	Department of Humanitarian Affairs (now OCHA)
DPA	Department of Political Affairs
DRR	Deputy Resident Representative (of UNDP)
ERD	Emergency Response Division
EU	European Union
FAO	Food and Agriculture Organization of the UN
GDP	gross domestic product
GTZ	Gesellschaft fur Technische Zusammenarbeit
HABITAT	United Nations Centre for Human Settlements
HC	Humanitarian Coordinator
IASC	Inter-Agency Standing Committee
ICAO	International Civil Aviation Organization
ICRC	International Committee of the Red Cross
IDP	internally displaced person
IFAD	International Fund for Agricultural Development
IGAD	Inter-Governmental Authority for Development
ILO	International Labour Organization
IOM	International Organization of Migration

IMF	International Monetary Fund
IRC	International Red Cross
JICA	Japan International Cooperation Agency
MSA	Miscellaneous Services Agreement
MoU	Memorandum of Understanding
NEX	national execution
OCHA	Office for the Coordination of Humanitarian Affairs
ODA	official development assistance
OECD	Organization for Economic Cooperation and Development
OSCE	Organization for Security and Cooperation in Europe
PMU	Project Management Unit
PRODERE	Development Programme for Displaced Persons, Refugees and Returnees in Central America
QIP	Quick Impact Project
RC	Resident Coordinator (of the UN)
RR	Resident Representative (of the UNDP)
RRDP	Rehabilitation, Reconstruction and Development Programme
RSS	reintegration support scheme
SFOR	Stabilization Force (international NATO-led peace keeping force)
SEILA	Not an acronym; it means "cornerstone" in Khmer
SHD	sustainable human development
SPR	special programme resources
SRSG	Special Representative of the Secretary-General
TRAC	Target for Resource Assignment from the Core
UNCDF	United Nations Capital Development Fund
UNCT	United Nations Country Team
UNDAF	United Nations Development Assistance Framework
UNDP	United Nations Development Programme
UNDPKO	United Nations Department of Peacekeeping Operations
UNESCO	United Nations Educational, Scientific and Cultural Organization
UNFPA	United Nations Population Fund
UNHCR	Office of the United Nations High Commissioner for Refugees
UNICEF	United Nations Children's Fund
UNMOT	United Nations Mission of Observers
UNOPS	United Nations Office for Project Services
UN RC	United Nations Resident Coordinator
UNSCERO	UN Special Coordinator for Emergency and Relief Operations
UNV	United Nations Volunteer Programme (or UN Volunteer)
USAID	U.S. Agency for International Development
WFP	World Food Programme
WHO	World Health Organization
WHO/PAHO	World Health Organization/Pan American Health Organization
WID	Women in Development

BIBLIOGRAPHY

Anderson, Mary B., *Do No Harm. How Aid can Support Peace or War*, London 1999

Apthorpe, R., "Kosovo Humanitarian Programme Evaluations: Towards Synthesis, Meta-Analysis and Sixteen Propositions for Discussion", Background Paper for ALNAP Symposium: Learning-from-Evaluation: Humanitarian Assistance and Protection in Kosovo, Overseas Development Institute, London, U.K., September 2000

Feinstein, O. & Picciotto, R., Eds., *Evaluation and Poverty Reduction – Proceedings from a World Bank Conference*, World Bank, Washington, D.C., 2000

Inter-Agency Standing Committee (IASC) Reference Group on Post-Conflict Reintegration, "Final Report", Geneva, Switzerland, November 2000

Kaufman, Daniel, *Governance and Anti-Corruption: New Insights and Challenges*, Proceedings from a World Bank Conference, World Bank, Washington, D.C., 2000

Muggah, R. & Berman, E., "Humanitarianism Under Threat: The Humanitarian Impacts of Small Arms and Light Weapons", A Study Commissioned by the Reference Group on Small Arms of the Inter-Agency Standing Committee, New York, NY, March 2001

OECD, "DAC Guidelines on Conflict, Peace and Development Co-operation", Paris, France, 1997

Stewart, Frances, *Tackling Horizontal Inequalities*, Proceedings from a World Bank Conference, World Bank, Washington, D.C., 2000

Stiefel, Matthias, *Rebuilding After War: Lessons from the War-torn Societies Project*, WSP, Geneva, Switzerland, 1999

United Nations, "Report of the Panel on United Nations Peace Operations", August 2000

UNDP Business Plans 2000-2003, "Role of UNDP in Crisis and Post-conflict Situations", DP/2001/4, Executive Board of UNDP and UNFPA, November 2000

UNDP Emergency Response Division, "Light Weapons and the Proliferation of Armed Conflicts", New York, NY, April 1999

UNDP Emergency Response Division, "Mainstreaming Governance and Conflict Prevention", Programme Support Document, New York, NY, 2001

UNDP Emergency Response Division & USAID Office of Transition Initiatives, "Community-Based Reintegration and Rehabilitation in Post-Conflict Settings", Washington, D. C., October 2000

UNDP Evaluation Office, *Sharing New Ground in Post-Conflict Situations – The Role of UNDP in Reintegration Programmes,* New York, NY, January 2000

UNDP-Ministry of Foreign Affairs of Japan Joint Evaluation, "Post-Conflict Assistance of the Government of Japan through UNDP in Kosovo and East Timor", New York, NY, June 2001

UNDP-UNHCR, "Evaluation of the UNDP/UNHCR Joint Reintegration Programming Unit in Rwanda", Kigali, Rwanda, October 2000

UN Executive Committee on Humanitarian Affairs (ECHA) Working Group on Disarmament, Demobilization and Reintegration, "Harnessing Institutional Capacities in Support of the Disarmament, Demobilization and Reintegration of Former Combatants", New York, NY, July 2000

UN General Assembly, Security Council, "Prevention of Armed Conflict", Report of the Secretary-General, A/55/985-S/2001/574, June 2001

World Bank Operational Manual, "Bank Procedures – Development Cooperation and Conflict", Washington, D. C., January 2001

World Bank Operational Manual, "Operational Policies – Development Cooperation and Conflict", Washington, D. C., January 2001

ABOUT THE EDITORS

Rafeeuddin Ahmed is an eminent development specialist whose long career with the United Nations included the posts of Chef de Cabinet of the Secretary-General, Under Secretary-General for International Economic and Social Affairs, Under Secretary-General for Political Affairs, Trusteeship and Decolonization, Special Representative of the Secretary-General for Humanitarian Affairs in South East Asia, Executive Secretary of the United Nations Economic and Social Commission for Asia and the Pacific, and Associate Administrator of UNDP.

Manfred Kulessa, a former UNDP resident representative and deputy regional director, is a distinguished development practitioner widely recognized for his contributions to development and the causes of humanity. In Germany, he served as Director of the German Development Service. Since his retirement, he has been active in consultancies and civil society groups, such as the Chairman of the German Asia Foundation.

Khalid Malik, Director of the UNDP Evaluation Office since 1997, previously served in a variety of key UNDP managerial, technical and policy positions, including UN Representative in Uzbekistan. Since 1998, Mr. Malik has also been instrumental in the introduction within UNDP of results based management, which is emerging as a critical factor in the reform of the organization. He chairs the UN Inter-Agency Group on Evaluation and, jointly with colleagues from the World Bank and key bilateral organizations, has helped shape the emerging evaluation agenda and contributed to the global debate on the development effectiveness of aid agencies.